THE GAZETTEER of DARTMOOR NAMES

BY MIKE BROWN

FOREST PUBLISHING

First published in 1995 by FOREST PUBLISHING, Woodstock, Liverton, Newton Abbot, Devon TQ12 6JJ

Copyright © Mike Brown 1995

All rights reserved. No part of this book may be reproduced or transmitted in any form or by any means, electronic or mechanical, including photocopying, recording or by any information storage or retrieval system, without written permission from the publisher.

British Library Cataloguing in Publication Data

A catalogue record for this book is available from the British Library.

ISBN 0-9515274-7-9

Forest Publishing

Editorial, design and layout by:
Mike Lang

Typeset by:
Carnaby Typesetting, Torquay, Devon TQ1 1EG

Printed and bound in Great Britain by:
BPC Wheatons Ltd, Exeter, Devon EX2 8RP

Cover Photographs:

Front – Looking across the valley of the West Dart towards Wistman's Wood and Longaford Tor
                                                    (Stewart Bergman)

Back – The White Lady Waterfall in Lydford Gorge
                                                    (Mike Lang)

CONTENTS

	Page
Introduction	4
The Gazetteer of Dartmoor Names	7
Appendix I: Prehistoric and Industrial Archaeology Sites	58
Appendix II: Some Useful Addresses and Telephone Numbers	61
Appendix III: The Country Code – How the visitor can help	62
Bibliography	63

ACKNOWLEDGEMENTS

To Steve McKeogh, Ted Fitch, Dave and Kath Brewer, Nancy van der Kiste and others who have provided information for this book.

INTRODUCTION

Welcome to the Gazetteer of Dartmoor Names, which I sincerely hope will be an extremely useful and informative source of reference to visitors and explorers of the moor, and to letterbox hunters alike.

This edition, which has been prepared exclusively for Forest Publishing, is, in fact, a revised and updated edition to that first published privately in 1993. However, apart from containing many more entries, this new edition also takes into account the changes made to the Dartmoor National Park boundary in 1994. In addition, I have now been able to include a supplement (Appendix I) providing, in grid square order, a list of prehistoric and industrial archaeology sites with the aim of providing even greater assistance to would-be 'explorers'.

It must be pointed out, however, that there are almost certainly many purely local names which are unknown to me, besides other names, sites and objects of interest (hopefully, no more than just a few!) that for one reason or another I may have overlooked. I must, therefore, ask users to appreciate that it is difficult for such a work ever to be considered as *complete*. Nevertheless, this new edition of The Gazetteer does contain more than *six thousand entries* — nearly twice as many names as will be found on the current O.S. 1:25,000 Outdoor Leisure Map 28, which covers the Dartmoor area!

In order that users may derive maximum benefit from this Gazetteer, I now include the following explanatory notes:

PLACE NAMES. The bulk of the entries in The Gazetteer comprise names which are in current usage for the location, feature or object, and historical variants and ancient forms have been excluded. Exceptions to this basic rule are those local and traditional names which have been used in the recent past, but which now have largely fallen out of general usage. The senior citizens of the Dartmoor parishes of today are probably the last generation who will use these centuries-old local names in their everyday speech, names of historical value which should be recorded before the modern age sweeps them away and they disappear altogether.

Some previous authors have made scathing remarks regarding the misspellings and corrupted forms of many modern Dartmoor names, but caution has to be exercised regarding the "correctness" of one spelling over another. For example, a farm in Buckland Parish has been variously named Puttesham, Puttisham, Putsome, Putstone, Putsam, Putshane, Putsham, Pudsham, Tapper's Putsham and Mead's Putsham in relatively recent times, so that although the name Higher Pudsham is correctly applied to it today, none of the other variants can strictly be described as being incorrect.

Notwithstanding the foregoing comment, there are a great many names on the current O.S. Outdoor Leisure Map 28 (the base map used) which are either misspelt or misplaced. All such sites are entered in The Gazetteer but are *not* given a grid reference, this being replaced by a bracketed cross-reference to the *correct name*. Please note, however, that in some instances two quite different names may be applied equally correctly to the same site, and in such instances the grid reference is given under both entries.

It should also be noted that in many instances two words of a feature can be combined to name others in the vicinity, and users should check for such possibilities when using The Gazetteer. For example, the two words of Hart Tor are combined in the nearby features of Hartor Corner, Hartor Ford, Hartor Hole, etc., and thus follow Harton in the strict alphabetical sequence.

CHRISTIAN NAMES ETC. Where personal names are applied to a site, the entry is under the initial letter of the full name, for the obvious reason that to do otherwise would totally destroy the meaning of the name. For example, Jimmie Pickles' Lane is listed under 'J', for entries such as "Lane, Jimmie Pickles'" or "Pickles', Lane, Jimmie" would look rather stupid and be totally meaningless! Similarly, names prefixed by Higher, Great, Upper etc., and also the compass points, are also listed under the initial letter of the full name. For example, North Creber is entered under 'N' rather than "Creber, North".

CROSSES. To avoid any possible confusion between carved granite crosses and cross roads, stone crosses are denoted with the suffix 'X', whilst road junctions are given the name "... Cross". An example where confusion could possibly occur is that of the stone Beetor X does not in fact stand at the Beetor Cross road junction.

ENCLOSURES & FIELDS. Every one of the many thousands of enclosed pieces of land on Dartmoor bears a name, all of which are obviously impossible to include. Entries in The Gazetteer are thus restricted to the larger newtakes, plus those other enclosures which contain features of archeological or historical interest.

INHABITED DWELLINGS, FARMS ETC. Again, obviously not all can be included (this is, after all, not the Yellow Pages!), but all buildings which have important historical or architectural features have been included in The Gazetteer, as have most of the inns and pubs.

UNKNOWN LOCATIONS. There are a few sites included in The Gazetteer for which accurate identification has not been possible, due to the vagueness of the description of the location in the book(s) consulted and the impossibility of identification in the field. Some, for which approximate locations are known, are entered with approximate grid references, thus: 67??69??; others have a grid reference followed by a query, "(?)", indicating that the grid reference given is the assumed one; a few are simply listed as "(?)". I hope that users will agree that this method is better than omitting such names altogether.

THE GRID REFERENCES THEMSELVES. These are 4-, 6-, or 8-figures, obviously dependant upon the size of the feature, and a few notes on these will help:

ALL LARGE EXPANSES OF MOORLAND (hills, commons, downs etc): 4-fig GR of the square approximately at the centre of the area.

ALL SMALLER LANDSCAPE FEATURES (tors, small hills, mires etc): 6- or 8-fig GRs, depending upon size and extent.

ALL LINEAR FEATURES (tracks, walls, reaves etc): 8-fig GR to *one end* of the feature, followed by a bracketed compass direction denoting the direction in which the feature runs (this avoids possible confusion at junctions).

WATERCOURSES: On Dartmoor most natural watercourses issue from a miry head, so 6-fig GRs are given, which indicate the approximate centre of the head of the river, brook or stream (note that this will be a very approximate location for large headmires and multiple heads). Where the GR is given in brackets, this denotes that the watercourse does not have a "head" in the accepted sense, but continues upstream under a different name. Regarding leats, all major leats have been included whether flowing or otherwise, the GR indicating the site of the headweir

ANCIENT & INDUSTRIAL ARCHAEOLOGY: 6- or 8-fig GRs, depending upon size and extent. Regarding industrial sites, users should note that most mining operations had widely scattered sites, and the grid reference entered in The Gazetteer indicates the main site or that with the most prominent ruins. Also, in some instances, the name of the mine has been included despite the fact that no visible features remain at the site today.

Finally, I must draw the users' attention to the Acknowledgments, for without the kind and generous help of these people some of the more obscure place-names would not have been correctly identified. To them, and to others who have contributed in any manner, I say a special 'thank you'.

Mike Brown
January 1995

THE GAZETTEER OF DARTMOOR NAMES

A

A Stone	62066728
Aaron's Knock (see Herring's Knock)	
Abbey Pool	74206755
Abbot's Gate	62516160
Ace of Diamonds	538745
Adams Hele	74357030
Addicombe	64755818
Ford	64375920
Path	64535762 (N)
Slaggets	647585
Addiscott	66709339
X	66699333
Addislade	71576405
Water	716643
Adley House	71048771
Aish	69156080
Bridge	69005990
Ridge	682609
Tor	702715
Aishridge Plantation	67856079
Albion Mine	782767
Alder Wood	789773
Alderpark Copse	78408967
Plantation	707873
Aller	74348318
Aller	80998011
Brook	675713
Brook Ford	67507183
Alston	77647200
Cross	77617135
Amicombe Bend	57848384
Hill	5786
Water	578856
Anchor Inn	69796013
Anderton Mine	485723
Anglers Rest	74348996
Annie Pinkham's Men	509814
Anthony Stile	58879260
Apton's Marsh	679648
Arch Tor	63367817
Archerton	63787921
Bog	629791
Bog Stream	629791
Brook	624804
(Braddon Lake on map)	
Newtake	6279
Arme Head Stone	62066728
Arms Tor	541863
Rings	536863
Arrishes	648726
Arrow Head Field	592740

Arthur Hill	562792
Arundel Mine (see Druid Mine)	
Asacombe Bottom	658827
Brook	658817
Gate	66078190
Hill	664821
House	65918263
Row	66058260
Ash (see Aysh)	
Ash Bridge	67819060
Farm	49407169
Green	664896
Green Gate	66498958
Ashburn River	752747
Ashburton	7569
Down	772725
Down Plantation	769724
Umber Mine	762704
United Mines	772735
Ashbury Hill	82068761
Hill Down	819875
Tor	60509405
Ashbury's, The	50608052
Ashlands	49367197
Ashleigh	49707152
Ashplants	74348996
Ashwell Lane	79887970 (E)
Assacombe Hill etc (see Asacombe...)	
Assycombe Hill etc (see Asacombe...)	
Atlas Mine	77857618
Aune Head	650695
Mires	649695
Ausewell	73497092
Common	735713
Corner	73337264
Cottages	73307250
Cross	73907205
Down	735713
Gate	73337264
Mine	728710
Rocks	731716
Wood	730715
Avenue, The	76187532 (SE)
Avon Cott	69056110
Dam	679652
Filtration Works	67566294
Ford	66446615
Reservoir	677653
River	650696
Axna	51288010
Aysh	66658966

B

Babeny	67187516
Gate	67297513
Green	673748
Mill	67297513
Rit	668748
Steps	67207470
Bachelor's Hall	60107360
Brook	598733
Mill	60107360
Mine	597735
Newtake	6173
Peat Works	601736 (?)
Badger's Holt	67297352
Badworthy (see Lower Badworthy)	
Bridge	68536180
Brook	677609
Leat	66556255
Bag Tor	76207575
Gert	764759
Mire	758765
Newtake	7575
Bagga Tor	54808058
Bridge	54508099
Brook	562817
Gate	54628053
Marsh	544811
Newtake	5580
Baggator Farm	54858090
Mine	550810
Bagley Wood	725734
Bagpark	72147832
Plantation	719784
Bagtor Barton	76567519
Cottages	76197552
Down	7575
Ford	76007563
Gate	76117599
Manor	76567519
Mill	76857550
Mine	76657583
Woods	762747
Bakers Arms (now Bullers Arms)	
Bakery Hill	601737
Bal Mine	56906931
Bala Brook	659648
Ford	67006301
Heath	6664
Leat	66646407
Ball Gate	67026129
Wood	678878
Balls	648915
Balls, The	666909
Balland	76737126
Barewalls	52908439
Barn Hill	533748
Barn House Barton (see Barnecourt)	
Barne	83138509
Cross	76258373
Barnecourt	75918441
Barnefield	75808455

Barnsey Bridge	75487046
Barnstaple Inn (now The Bay Horse Inn)	
Barrack Gate	59077350
Barracks, The	65697113
	64827879
Barracott	73528169
Lane	72998180
Mine	740822
Barramoor Bog	714837
Bridge	71758341
Brook	(717829)
Farm	71718345
Barren Corner	71257110
Barrett's Bridge	51238206
Barrow Way Cross	67318960
Barton Down	829830
Batch Loaves, The	71257147
Batten's Corner	47458123
Steps	48507976 (?)
Battishill Down	515857
Battleship Island	64717348
Batworthy	66098660
Batworthy	71478525
Brook	661864
Common	6586
Cross	70828544
Inner Mire (see Batworthy Mires)	
Mill	71348520
Mill Cross	70838547
Mires	653868
Bawden's Bungalow	67548106
Bay Horse Inn	75507000
Beach Holt	63888200
Beacon Cottages	73007291
Down	797861
Hill	736726
Lane	82278083 (SE)
Plain	6659
Plantation	732732
Plantation	809851
Rocks	66855911
Beadon	81598169
Bridge	81778189
Cottage	81568136
Cross	81558110
Beara	659888
Beara	663892
Common	703614
House	66187231
Meadow	658727
Mill (see The Mill)	
Plantation	720739
Bearas, The	660727
Beardon Farm	51828421
Gate	52078398
Beardown	6076
Bridge	60317530
Brook	598777
Clapper	60257534
Farm	60437542

Beardown Hill	603759
Lodge	60447505
Man	59617962
Newtake	6077
Newtake Corner	59227835
Tors	6077
Warren	600755
Bearland	74328530
Bearslake Inn	52838888
Bearwalls (see Barewalls)	
Beatland Corner	54826240
X	54826240
Beatrice Chase, grave of	71897679
Becka Brook	738768
Falls	76188008
Ford	75617996
Beckaford	76127962
Bridge	75617996
Beckamoor Brook (see Beckamoor Water)	
Combe	536748
X	53477430
Dip	536761
Ford	53767472
Water	535760
Beckhams	76258049
Tree Cross	83788360
Becky Brook etc (see Becka...)	
Bedford Bridge	50407035
House	50497040
Bee Tor	70828440
Beechcroft Plantation	559685
Beechlands	69408765
Beehive Combe	66607290
Beesleigh Copse	827833
Beetor Bridge	70858505
Cross	71308430
X	71308419
Farm	71108442
Beggar's Bush	695593
Bel Tor	697730
Corner	69507312
Belford Mill	75357153
Bell Inn	75378604
Lane	82278083 (E)
Tor	73057785
Bellever	655774
Bridge	65837732
Combe	651768
Combe Lake	648760
Combe Stream	648760
Newtake	6576
Tor	644764
Belpool Island	69917130
Belson	571819
Belstone	620936
Bible	68357386
Chair	68607411
Cleave	626935
Common	6192
Consols Mine	627934
Pound (see Halstock Pound)	
Ridge	6192

Belstone Tors	6192
Belt, The	747734
Belter's Ford	64206502
Beltor Bog	734778
Mires	734778
Stream	733774
Bench Tor (see Benjy Tor)	
Benet's X	68058170
Benjy Tor	691716
Bennett's Reservoir	516796
Berra Tor	55206790
Berra Tor	47816906
Berricky Ford	64076103
Berry Cross	80778993
Down (see Berrydown)	
Pound	713803
Berrydown Farm	66548790
Gate	66368793
Stroll	662878
Bert Gratton's Hut	64269007
Bethel Cross	78227427
Bethelcombe Cross	78727435
Bicklime Wood	536712
Biera Wood	704876
Big Covert	832827
Gate	62338455
Head	58257315
Pond	575632
Rock	527799
Rock	73997771
Shed	58416624
Whit Hill	6390
(named White Hill on map and slightly misplaced)	
Bigport Farm	79098985
Bilberry Hill	72706680
Bilberryhill Copse	722670
Biller's Pound	66706617
Billy's Tor	56737450
Binkham Farm	52436850
Binnamore	68696142
Cross	68736141
Birch	82278732
Cleave Wood	827826
Down	816873
Pool	73326811
Tor	687814
Tor Inn (now Headland Warren Farm)	
Tor & Vitifer Mine	681810
Tor & Vitifer Mine Leat	62528118
Birchanger Cross (see Burchanger Cross)	
Birchcleave House	49797076
Birchey	50497280
Birchy Lake	61999310
Birchy Lake	618929
Gate	62049298
Birkham Ford & Gate (see Burcombe...)	
Bishop's Meads	667659
Stone	78588152
Bittaford	666570
Bridge	66615699
Bittleford	70567490

Bittleford Down	707756
Gate	70707507
Blachford Leat	62596142
Manor	61255996
Saw Mill	61626002
Black Beam	664679
Brake	683631
Brook Farm	58847498
Bush	671677
Down	5891
Down	694785
Down	5082
Down village (see Blackdown)	
Dunghill	581774
Dunghill Stream	585777
Fen	673832
Furzes (see Blakey Furzes)	
Hill	761786
Hill	604846
Hill	523825
Hole	582845
Hole	573781
Hole Crossing-Place	57317820
Hut	64586783
Lane (N)	55878030 (NE)
Lane (S)	62706944 (S)
Pool	68507199
Pool	65495812
Pool Island	73046841
Prince's Tomb	63599315 (?)
Ridge	595855
Ridge Brook (see Black Ridge Water)	
Ridge Cut (see Black Ridge Peat Pass)	
Ridge Peat Pass	598859 (S)
Ridge Water	602850
Rock	57107804
Rock	53507599
Rock	533853
Rock Falls	53308531
Rock Quarry (see Bullycleaves Quarry)	
Rock Valley	571780
Rocks	65535832
Rocks	62956705
Shells	51707825
Stubbs Plantation	723699
Swan (now Three Crowns)	
Tor	567895
Tor	573718
Tor	681635
Tor Beare	567890
Tor Falls	57407149
Tor Ford	57507166
Tor Hole	57407149
Tor Mire	680641
Tor Rings	680633
Black's Newtake	638760
Black-a-Tor Copse	567890
Blacka Brook	574634
Blacka Brook	580778
Blacka Brook	550707
Blacka Tor	68107830 (?)
Blacka Tor	69437850
Blackabrook Bridge	58807498
Head	583782
Blackadon (see Blackaton Manor)	
Down	714733
Farm	66555769
Lane	71387272 (N)
Tor	712734
Blackaller	73758381
Quarry	729912
Blackaton	69508020
Ball	694785
Bridge	69567783
Bridge	67718882
Brook	640900
Cross	67838899
Cross	69767782
X	67808905
X	57056310
Down	7078
Hole	64859092
Manor	69367773
Newtake	703786
Quarry Ford	64269007
Slaggets	572632
Blackator Mead	666750
Rocks	66697500
Blackaven Brook	592885
Blackdown	503797
Inn (now Royal Standard)	
Blackey Tor	61287366
Blackhay (see Jobbers)	
Blackhole Plantation	78488970
Blackingstone	79208559
Farm	78568327
Quarry	78358580
Rock	78648559
Blackland Corner	62785938
Blacklands	537640
Brook	538653
Mire	542649
Blacklane Brook (see Wollake)	
Brook Ford (see Wollake Ford)	
Ford	63036802
Mire	630683
Mire Stream	633683
Blackman's Holt	68206478
Blackmoor	73666831
Water	738681
Wood	732685
Blackpool	81277406
Head	83208720
Island	73036842
Blackrock Pool	74416673
Blackslade	72747559
Down	734756
Ford	73607519
Mire	738756
Newtake (see Kingswell Newtake)	
Water	740758
Blacksmith's Shop	53587473
Blacksmith's Shop	75787627
Blacksmith's Shop	63808426

Blacksmith's Shop	58936986
Blacksmith's Shop	68198095
Blackstone	64008602
Blackwood Path	64206502 (N)
Blakedon Pipard	69347951
Blakey Furze Pool	64767383
Blakey Furzes	649738
Tor	61307366
Bleak House	55988648
Bleak House	50927258
Bledge Brook	628646
Ford	63106421
Hill	634645
Blindwell Plantation	549693 (?)
Blissmoor	73798063
Brook	735804
Bloody Pool	70296262
Brake	703628
Blowing Stone	52437383
Blue Burrows	589710
Gate	69677890
Jug	70828037
Post (see Blue Stone)	
Stone	70757760
Board'n House	60997568
Boathill	76368565
Boiler, The	624711
Boldventure	67298614
Newtake	67298614
Bonehill (see Higher and Lower Bonehill)	
Bonehill	72557750
Down	734776
Gate	73157758
House	72327750
Lawn	731775
Rocks	73157745
Boro Wood	752715
Camp	749716
Bot Tor	82708050
Bottlehill Leat (see Lee Moor Leat)	
Bottomoclose Plantation	801763
Bottor	82538016
Rock	82708050
Bottor's Nose	82538016
Boulter's Tor	52507806
Boundstone	65946965
Bourne's Pit	66196920
Bovey Bridge	73778372
Combe	765812
Combe Cliff	768415
Combe Head	677818
Cross	74328470
River	677818
(misnamed N Wallabrook on map)	
Rock	73387668
Bow Combe	618477
Ford	62068811
Hill	616866
Mire	618477
Bowbeer	71909118
Bowda	74008312
Bowden	82258459
Bowden	70056720
Bowden	72707365
Ball	71769037
Barn	71297676
Beer	825847
Farm	71989070
Farm	72608372
Farm	74758801
Hill Iron Mine	(?)
Lane	73207350 (W)
Mill	72458404
Plantation	544669
Bowdley Plantation	746716
Bowdown Cross	72436254
Bowerdon	70836659
Bowerman's Nose	74148047
Bowling Green	545626
Boyland	79318942
Boyton	50547183
Bracken Tor	58849386
Braddon Lake (see Archerton Brook)	
Tor	62257990
Bradford Pool	700910
Bradmere Pool	700910
Brady Park	826801
Brag Lane	547632
End	54436306
Brai Tor	53988557
Brake	682811
Brake, The	681879
The	76259250
Corner	70207163
Plantation	669743
Brandiron Cross	83408092
Branscombe's Loaf (see Bronescombe's Loaf)	
Brat Tor (see Brai Tor)	
Breast-The-Water	522814
Brenamoor Common	623939
Brent (see South Brent)	
Bridge	69735955
Fore Hill	667618
Hill	704617
Mill	69725967
Moor	6763
Moor Clay Works	67956288
Moor House	68296350
Moor House Warren	681634
Moor Naptha Works	67956288
Rings (see Ryder's Rings)	
Tor	471804
Tor Down	70?61?
Brentor	482814
Brian's Lane	65109154 (E)
Gate	65109154
Bridestowe & Sourton Common	5588
Bridford	816864
Bridge	83408720
Wood	804881
Bridfordmills	83518701
Bridge	72487307
Bridge	50908444
Farm	60765919

Name	Ref
Brim Brook	594882
Park Ford	64307394
Park Pool	64317395
Brimbley Ford	66986926
Brimhill Lane	51808002 (SW)
Tor	51857948
Brimley Farm	80107702
Lane	79437641 (NE)
Brimpts	666740
Farm	66837389
Gate	66537343
Little Newtake	666750
Mead	672735
Mine	652747
Mine Leat	635?764?
Newtake Stream	663746
Northern Wood	671746
Outer Newtake	660748
Plantations	6674
Wood	6674
Brimstone Down	666871
Brimstonedown	66808730
Brinning	75258501
Brinsabach	48207980
Brisery Burrows etc (see Brisworthy…)	
Brisworthy	56006520
Brook	560653
Burrows	563645
Circle	56486550
Mire	560653
Plantation	556657
Broad Amicombe Hole	578863
Barrow	70577987
Burrow	70577987
Combe	80037730
Down	626804
Down Brook (see Archerton Brook)	
Down Ring (see Broadun Ring)	
Falls	65316701
Hole	59157860
Marsh (see Broada Marsh)	
Mead	6167
Moor	684598
Moor	526785
Moor Bottom	694838
Oak	613821
Rock	61816724
Rushes	665648
Stone	65118927
Broada Marsh	618819
Marsh Stream	614810
Stones	618819
Broadaford	69307623
Brook	703791
Broadall Down	6163
Gulf	607640
Lake	606639
Leat	60816337
Broadalls	70548609
Broadmoor	690833
Brook	546795
Common	757899
Broadmoor Common	688830
Cottage	75509059
Farm	52737856
Mires (see Metheral Bog)	
Broadstone	68907233
Broadun	6280
Enclosure	635799
Hole	67358143
Newtake	6380
Pound	635799
Ring	637802
Rocks	632806
Broady Well	659665
Brock Hill	674662
Ford	67906580
Mires	678663
Stream	679661
Brockenborough	61807196
Brockhill Wood	542719
Brockley Bottom	675705
Brokers Plantation	601612
Bronescombe's Loaf	55208915
Brook	52497126
Barn	62626006
Cottage	66488940
Farm	71206780
Hill	632893
House	52607103
Manor	71316769
Mill	72396747
Wood	710672
Brook's Head	571820
Brookfield	78858150
Brookland	75567075
Brookwood Mine	718675
Broom Mead	642752
Park	64357391
Park Pool	64307400
Broomhill	53337248
Broomhill	63775854
Leat	64095918
Reservoir	646593
Broomspire Park Copse	768918
Brousentor Farm	54518067
Gate	54558062
Lane	54558062 (NW)
Brown Heath	640660
Hill	648791
Brownberry (misplaced on map)	64707445
Newtake	649746
Wood	646742
Browne's House	61507987
Bog	614794
Stream	615798
Brownsdon Tor Farm (see Brousentor…)	
Bryher	54156909
Bubhill Mine	607915
Buckfast	739673
Abbey	741673
Buckfastleigh	7366
Moor	677678
Buckland Beacon	73507310

Buckland Bridge	71897195
Common	7373
Court	72087300
Ford	65966604
Ford Water	659659
Hall	73237259
Woods	730715
Buckland-in-the-Moor	721731
Bucktor	48026989
Buda	69188665
Budbrooke	75499231
Lane	75429240 (S)
Buddla Corner	52918164
Lane	52578075 (N) (?)
Budleigh Bridge	76258544
Bude X	63129477
Lane	63129477 (E)
Bugshead Cross	73418540
X	73418540
Bulkamore Iron Mine	(?)
Bull Park	607733
Ring, The	56056759
Buller's Arms (now Mary Tavy Inn)	
Buller's Arms	69998757
Bullpark	60287331
Bullaton Cross	80458230
Farm	80108205
Rock	79628220
Bullaven	64015980
Bullhornstone Cross	68366023
Farm	67906002
Bullycleaves Quarry	742667
Bungalow Firs	581673
Burchanger Brake	770754
Cross	77287557
Burchetts Wood	721679
Burcombe Bridge	57906731
Ford	57906731
Gate	57776738 (?)
Burford Down	637603
Burham	53906955
Burn, The	634606
Burn, The	710810
Burn Lane	48198217 (SE)
Lane Path	50658090 (N) (?)
Plain	5077
Burnford	49567872
Burnicombe	80108734
Down	803870
Burnville	48908247

Burra Tor (see Berra Tor)	
Burracombe Ford & Gate (see Burcombe...)	
Burrator Dam	55156801
Falls	55206758
Gorge	551679
Halt	54976785
House	55506771
Inn	53706888
Lawn (see The Lawn)	
Lodge	55196853
Pits	55506763
Reservoir	5568
Wood	552675
Burrough Farm	74879100
Burrow Corner	73607522
Cleave	565923
Bush Down	682823
Down Heath (see Bush Down)	
Down Mine	681819
Down Stream	687823
Meads	654659
Pits	660652
Pool	66007292
Butte Park	71847681
Butter Brook	651598
Ford	64375920
Butterburies Hedges	5579
Newtake	5579
Butterdon	75278802
Ball Wood	7589
Down	750884
Hill	656587
Hill	75278802
Rifle Range	655602
Stone Row	65625880 (N)
Buttern	65758939
Circle	64948849
Hill	653885
Lane	65778950 (S)
Rocks (see Buttern Tor)	
Tor	65308868
Button	71856718
Wood	724673
Butts Cross	71646391
By The Down	52357225
Byes, The	660730
Byhead Turnpike	70078324
Byland	74627062
Bymore Wood	485701
Byteign Lodge	84168391

C

Cadaford	55526461
Bridge (see Cadover Bridge)	
Cadover Bridge	55526462
X	55316470
Cadworthy Farm (see Lower Cadworthy Farm)	
Tor	54216418
Wood	544641
Callisham	53706685
Down	538662

Callisham Ford	53806694
Lane	53846717 (S)
Tor	53806640
Calves Lake	608677
Calveslake Hill	609673
Tor	60816761
Camp, The	60409415
Canna	73288139
Park	71958313

Canonteign Barton	83788309
Down	830820
Falls	83208243
House	83548286
Cantrel	66035680
Clay Works	658566
Hill (see Western Beacon)	
Gate	65825718
Siding	65955730
Cape Horn	67228069
Captain Hunter Memorial	53308531
Carew Arms (now Woodpecker Inn)	
Caroline Bog	666811
Bottom	667808
Farm (see Wheal Caroline)	
Wheal Prosper	70166585
Carpenter's Arms	78597610
Wood	509804
Carrapitt	80058620
Carrington Memorial	54006420
Carrion Pool	58416624
Cascades, The	69867089
Casely Cleave	783820
Court	78608210
Wood	788825
Caseytown	50507320
Castle, The	59807173
Castle Cottage	72299042
Drogo	723901
Hill	683836
Inn	51008479
Park	66807861
Road	59107351 (S)
Castor Copse	801817
Rock (see Kes Tor)	
Cataloo Steps	54008112
Caters Beam	6368
Cathanger Rock	68507492
"Cathedral of the Moor"	71897679
Caton	78157187
Cator	68827626
Bog	672781
Common	674777
Court	68287698
Gate	68077633
Pound	67307767
Catstor Down	543659
Cattle Park (see Tor Royal Newtake)	
Cave-Penney Memorial	68357436
Caw's Mill (see Cole's Mill)	
Cawsand (see Cosdon)	
Cemetery, The	643916
Central Devon United Mine (see Devon United Mine)	
Chaffe's Newtake	657722
Chagford	701875
Bridge	69368795
Common	6783
Cross	75028643
Cross	68828830
House	70338740
Mill	69358783

Chalk Ford	68506810
Challacombe	69307949
Bottom	694800
Bridge	69427959
Cottages	69387961
Cross	69498306
Down	6880
Mine	69408019
Stone Row	690808
Challamoor	72397420
Chants Hill	594710
Chapel Ford	60809344
Lands	605934
Lands	58?73?
Lands Spring	60509338
Lane	51407760 (E)
of La Wallen	66948892
Chapple	67128912
Chapple	80027765
Brook	671890
Cross	67188902
Charles X	74268954
Wood	744895
Charlie's Rocks	68507492
Chase Gate	69737000
Hill	725705
House (see Holne Chase Hotel)	
Mine	723715
Wood	7271
Chasegate	71717049
Chat Tor	55538528
Chaw Gully	688809
Chericombe Head	82288083
Cheriton Combe	645913
Combe Water	644915
Cross	773930
Hill	642906
Cherrybrook	619802
Farm (now Cherrybrook Hotel)	
Hotel	62157600
Cheston	681586
Cross	68085860
Childe's Tomb	62407018
Chilly Wood	530805
Chimney Bow	622883
Chinkwell Tor	728781
Chipstone	558?680?
Chittaford Down	636794
Chittleford	72207571
Gate (see Chittleford Green Gate)	
Green	72887504
Green Gate	72887504
Cholake	617729
Cholwell	51308156
Brook	521817
Cholwichtown Leat	60??63??
Reave	59976251 (NW)
Chris Swanson Memorial	56427631
Christow	835848
Bridge	83738670
Common	823853
Chub Tor	52006610

14

Chubstone Wood	559681 (?)
Chudleigh Lodge	83758271
Church Cross	73916660
Ford	53026756
Hill	679752
House Inn	70606951
House Inn (now Walkhampton Church House)	
Lane	53238005 (N)
Lane	71157690 (E)
Lane Head	71157690
Lane Head	71217521
Path	(69727558) (NE)
Path	55906754 (W)
Path	58056659 (WNW)
Path	67957490 (NE)
Pool	66107299
Rock	558?753?
Steps	53646996
Wall	69177308 (W)
Way	66377305 (NE)
Way	66887848 (E)
Way	(67237318) (E)
Church of St. (see churches section under Saint (St))	
Claig Tor	54946759
Clam, The	74296731
Meadow	569700
Clambridge	76728109
Clampit's Stile	72206321
Clampitt	81028450
Down	815841
House	81438461
Plantation	815845
Clannaborough	66109120
Copse	66209150
Down	650909
Wood	664917
Claret Tor	66525872
Clarke's Barn Plantation	692681
Clay Brake	66507255
Tor	568781
Clay Works Leat (see Lee Moor Leat)	
Claypit Mires	669856
Claytor Moor	5678
Clazywell Pool etc (see Crazywell...)	
Cleag Tor	54946759
Clearbrook	525656
Cleava Ford	57786829 (?)
Gate	57786829 (?)
Cleave	72228690
Cleave, The	78548126
Brake	66507255
Combe	66607290
House	82958450
House	61209401
Mill	63899405
Mill	63839410
Rocks	60909408
Tor	60909408
Wood	711703
Wood	703737

Cleave Wood	722871
Cleft Rock	72697091
Click Tor	54946759
Clifford Barton	78069001
Bridge	78108977
Bridge Park	782897
Cottages	77598956
Farm	78068969
Clithers	68718326
Clove Stone Rock	73207827
Coad's Wood	518792
Coal Mires	6680
Coal Mires	713784
Coalmoor Head	713784
Coatmoor Hill	693703
Cockingford	71697501
Bridge	71707508
Mill	71707508
Cockle's Gate	57837006
Cockler's Peep Inn	67907491
Cocks Hill	569790
Lake	653744
Tor	531762
Cocksland Bridge	77707440
Cockstor Hill	531762
Cod Wood	788887
Coffin Mill	75417062
Stone	67707329
Wood	540810
Cold East Cross	74067420
Parks	661722
Colden Tor	61307366
Cole's Mill	59376676
Colehayes Park	79127760
Colehay's Plantation	795779
Coleridge Wood	777889
Colesworthy	80307565
Cross	80647589
Collabridge	80458975
Collaton Lane	52307543 (W)
Down	526755
Down Gate	52307542
Collard Tor	557621
Colleytown Farm (see Collyton)	
Colliers	58277015
Collihole	68508561
Colly Brook (see Peter Tavy Brook or Wedlake)	
Collyton	56506742
Collytown (see Collyton)	
Gate	56776725
Combe	83708395
Combe	78008180
Combe	78857402
Combe	70606808
Combe (see West Combe)	
Bridge	70316810
Brook	624626
X (see Higher Combe X)	
Down	543884
Edge	778819
Farm	61816107

Combe Gate	68207865
Head (see Curlicombe Brook)	
Head	677818
Hill	623630
Vale	721897
Wood	729726
Waste	619620
(see East and West Combe)	
Combeshead Bridge	58576848
Brake	645587
Brook	592692
Cross	63915828
Farm	58576855
Ford	58596848
Gert	593693
Tor	587688
Combestone Tor etc (see Cumston...)	
Combewear Hill	663727
Pool	66577256
Common Wood	522797
Common Wood	537641
Conchies' Road	60387323 (E)
Condyshull (see Conies Down)	
Conies Down	582792
Tor	58927910
Water	585788
Coombe	71357711
Coombe	67458891
Coombe	72028965
Copse	681873
Court	75458701
Down	7082
Down	543885
Farm	77468702
Gate	70918250
Hall	76129123
Head	704817
Newtake	702819
Tor	68588718
Wood	729726
Copper Hill Mine	(?)
Copplestone Farm	82088800
Down	816875
Corfield Ford	65966969
Corn Hole	555898
Ridge	5688
Corndon	69707450
Down	6874
Tors	687742
Wood	699747
Corndonford Farm	69267451
Corner Close	74397620
Cornishes	74306690
Cornsclose	69195950
Cornwood	606597
Inn	60555969
Maidens	63216205 (N)
Coronation Plantation	715722
Corpse Lane	53998112 (N)
Corringdon Ball etc (see Coryndon...)	
Coryndon	67596035
Ball	671609
Coryndon Ball Plantation	666609
Ford	66926002
Gate	66936002
Leat	66356153
Wood	671601
Cosdon	6391
Beacon	636915
Brook (see Forder Brook)	
House	63609149
Cossick	77708620
Cross	77378612
Cot, The	77657724
Cottamoor Cross	77017680
Counting House	55476475
Court Barton	83218560
Cow Bridge	66148642
Cowflop Bottom	614814
Cowsic End	607752
Fork	59137845
Gorge	604753
Head Ford	59338040
River	594805
Cox Lake	653744
Lake Bridge	65217405
Lake Combe	653743
Lake Longhouse (see The School House)	
Tor (see Cocks Tor)	
Cox Tor Gate	52187625
Tor Lane	52187625 (W)
Cox's Meadow	65157405
Newtakes	652744
Coxland	77937462
Coxtor Cross	51637617
Farm	52147614
Gate	52177623
Cracker Stone	64206641
Crad Hole	679661
Ring	67906610
Cramber Down	5871
Gert	589710
Pool	58957112
Tor	58367118
Cranbrook	74518880
Castle	739890
Down	740891
Crandford Bridge	534873
Brook	534873
Crane Hill	622690
Hill House	60696835
Lake	605685
Lake (see Smith Hill Brook)	
Mine	607683
Cranery, The	6576
Bottom	656770
Brook (see Bellever Combe Lake)	
Cranford Bridge	52608800
Brook	534873
Cranmere Pool	603858
Crazywell Cross	58307041
Bridge	58347057
Farm	58097005
Gert	582703

Crazywell Hill 583704
    Pool 582705
Creaber (see North and South Creber)
Brook (see Meavy Pool)
Creaber's Hole (see Creber's Hole)
Creason 52658060
    Wood 530801
Creber Farms (see North and South Creber)
    Pound 663881
    Stroll 661880
Creber's Hole 558917
    Rock 66525872
Crip Tor 56157312
    Farm 55597274
Cripdon 73418099
    Down 734805
    Gate 73388092
    Newtake 737807
Criptor 55577274
Crock of Gold 61427306
Crocker's Pits 561893
Crockern Cottage (see Parson's Cottage)
    Farm 61007570
    Tor 61567577
Crockerntor 61567577
Crockernwell 753924
Crocombe Bridge 84668115
Crofts Plantation 560696
Crooked Oak .... 643?618?
    Stone 73787496
Cross Farm 72809069
    Furzes 69886680
    Gate 70107531
    Gates 56166949
    Park 778825
    Park Cottage 67218969
    Tree 75488604
Cross-Taw 62129339
"Crossing" (house) 50548050
Crossing-Place 71337815
Crossways 65016588
Crossways 51907765
Crossways .... 51907765 (W)
Crow Tor 60707871
Crow's Buttress (see Raven Buttress)

Dagger Hill 678802
    Mine Leat 67778078
    Wheel 68338012
Dale's Brake .... 69157436 (?)
Dancers, The 63506442
Dark Lake (see Wollake)
Dart Bridge 74486672
    Gorge .... 6772 etc
    Head Cut .... 614850 (E)
    Hole 604787
    Hole 606785
    Leat Mine .... (?)
    River (see East Dart, West Dart,
        Double Dart)
    Vale 74097037

Crowder Park 705597
Crown Corner 67907544
    Hall Corner 65328529
    Hall Stream 654851
Crownley Parks 768757
Cuckoo Ball 661581
    Ball Corner 65955821
    Rock 58486871
    Rock (see Tristis Rock)
    Stone (see Buttern Tor)
Cuckoofield 71048819
Cuddyford Bridge 75807093
    Cross 75737093
Cudlipptown 521790
    Down 5379
    Lane .... 53107880 (W)
    Moorgate 53107880
Cullaford Bridge 70816790
Cullaton 68608632
Cullender 78637793
Cullever Steps 60609210
Cullicombe Head (see Curlicombe Brook)
Culverhouse 74007555
Cumston Farm 67007250
    Island 67387230
    Mine 672723
    Tor 670718
    Tor Hill 670718
    Track .... 67007176 (S)
    Wood 672723
Curbeam 559857
Curlicombe Brook 693822
    (misnamed East Bovey on map)
Curtery Clitters 593898
    (slightly misplaced on map)
    Stump 59068962
Cut Combe 592834
    Combe Water 593827
    Hill 598827
    Hill Stream 600820
    (name misplaced on map)
    Lane .... 59988321 (W)
    Lane Stream 603832
    (mis-named Cut Hill Stream on map)

D

Dartmeet 67137318
    Bridge 67197318
    Clapper 67197319
    Cottage (see Badger's Holt)
    Hill 675733
Dartmoor Consols 598682
    Gate 52498535
    Gate 70638202
    Gate 60359318
    Inn 54907520
    Inn 52308522
    Lane .... 64829322 (W)
    Path .... 56138510 (SW) and
    Path .... 51328227 (NE & SW)
    Prison 587741

Daveytown	54977320
Daw's Corner	56297074 (?)
Newtake	559795
Dead Lake	576706
Dead Lake	555846
Dead Lake	566785
Ford	55968413
Ford	56587848
Head	555848
Mire	558844
Pits	56587820
Well	555848
Deadlake Gert	57207035
Deadman's Bottom	609669
Bottom Stream	611672
Corner	70557046
Gulch	(?)
Deal	75508071
Copse	761801
Cottage	75418064
Deal's Bottom	675585
Brake	67465855
Dean Burn	682672
Burn Bridge	73276514
Burn Clapper	69826653
Clatters	711649
Cross	72016285
Moor	683657
Prior	72956350
Valley	7065 etc
Wood	715646
Deancombe	72256435
Brook	592683
Farm	57926879
Ford	57866868
Gert	587682
Lane	57926879 (W)
Marsh	592683
Deave Lane	67228967
Deep Bottom	554828
Huddit	58??68??
Swincombe	645714
Valley	541892
Deeper Marsh	714712
Pound	71397131
Deer Park Corner	67728407
Delamore House	60075992
Dendles Green	614618
Waste (see Hawns & Dendles)	
Wood	616619
Dene Nurseries	688588
Dennis Park	70408710
Dennithorne	52447500
Devil's Bridge	58057288
Bridge Hill	586732
Cauldron	50858457
Elbow	59077349
Frying-pan	56307687
Gully	582732
Kitchen	55498320
Point	54988300
Punchbowl	64207995

Devil's Rock	53886380
Tor	59697962
Devon & Courtenay Consols	49397054
Burra Mine	51427417
Friendship Leat (see Wheal Friendship Leat)	
Friendship Mine	506794
New Copper Mine (see Druid Mine)	
Tin Mine	668738
Tors	52096794
Union Mine	505766
United Mines	512786
Wheal Francis	783783
Wheal Vor	670670
Devonport Leat	60887796 and 59567677
Aquaduct	53846719
Dewerstone	53886380
Bridge	53496432
Cottage	53506432
Gorge	537636
Hill	539640
Rock	53886380
Tramway Incline	53706427 (S)
Wood	537637
Diamond Lane	67946230 (SW)
Dick's Well	55128605
Pits	547859
Dickford Bridge	74818370
Water	758837
Didworthy	685622
Bottom	682626
Bridge	68286212
Cottages	78208549
Turn	68266207
Dimps	53657710
Dinah's House	68458002
Dinger Plain	5889
Pool	58488950
Ridge	583885
Tor	58628810
Dinna Clerks	69??75??
Dinnaton	62015728
Dinnwell	67309305
Dip-trough Gate	62586142
Dippy Copse	79208962
Dishcombe	65989345
Ditsworthy Bungalow	58096731
Carriage-drive	57956628 (W)
Firs	580673
Ford	58216607
Gert	57956620
Warren	5866
(name slightly mis-placed on map)	
Warren House	58406628
Weir	58716620
Dittisham Wood	539712
Divides	62757299
Doccombe	77608681
Cross	77318645
Dockwell	69846372
Bottom	697635
Brake	698641

Dockwell Gate	69576359
Hole	697643
Plantation	698639
Pound	69726408
Ridge	6863
Stroll	695636
Doe Tor	542848
Bend	54508510
Bottom	536845
Brook	551860
Common	537846
Falls	535851
Farm	53658490
Gate	52??84??
Gate Ford	52808471
Gate Pool	52758470
Green	534852 (?)
Marsh	530848
Dog Pit	58416629
Dog Pit	56706476
Dogamarsh Bridge	71308931
Wood	710892
Doghole Bridge	84278170
Dogmarsh Bridge (see Dogamarsh Bridge)	
Dolly Trebble's House	64337255
Dolly's Cot	67217440
Donkey's Cave	77??815?
Corner	66418935
Double Dart	(67207310)
Waters	574729 and 584733
Waters	47606990
Waters Foot	578722
Dousland	537688
Barn (see Burrator Inn)	
Halt	53706882
Down Farm	53916650
Lane	52078398
Pool	52598185
Ridge	6571
Tor	580694
Tor Stone Row (misnomer – actually stands on Hingston Hill)	
Town Gate	52348560
Downes	69428562
Downfield Cottages	53347287
Downhouse	51107286
Downing's House	63956293
Brook	638629
Downpark	70978608
Downstow (see Higher Downstow)	
Cross	69206252
DPA Memorial Plaque	62497113
Dr. Blackall's Drive	64987268 (E)
Drake's Leat (see Plymouth Leat)	
Drakeford Bridge	78958013
Drascombe Barton	70179201
Dream Tor	77097678
Drewe Arms	73599088
Drewsteignton	736909
Cottages	731911
Cromlech (see Spinster's Rock)	
Drewston	726874

Drewston Common	738900
Cross	72078757
House	74259080
Wood	741902
Drift Court	67036128
Gate	68608341
Gate	64307933
Lane	68428334 (E)
Lane	64307933(S)
Drivage Bottom (misplaced on map)	597699
Stream	599699
Hut	59916993
Drizzlecombe (see Thrushelcombe)	
Druid	74407111
Arms (now Drewe Arms)	
Cottage	74707132
Cross	74337079
Farm	74307112
Mine	745715
Plantations	742714
Druid's Altar	78??85??
Well	71628621
Drum, The	57726449
Drury Brook	657796
Dry Bridge	74007450
Brook	677642
Lake	646639
Lake (Erme Head) (see Hux Lake)	
Lake Ford	63406639
Lake Rocks	633664
Lakes	660704
Lakes Gert	661707
Drywell	70007526
Cross	70107531
X	70107531
Duchy Hotel	59017349
Ducksmoor Cottage	78328730
Duckspool	624679
House	62786797
Stream	62806800
Ducky Pool	61879130
Duke Stone	74577726
Duke of Bedford's Leat (see Wheal Fortune Leat)	
Duke of Cornwall Consolidated Tin Mine	668738
Duke of Wellington's Nose	51596717
Duke's Nose	73017156
Dungeon, The	646622
Dunna Brook	642752
Dunnabridge	64457460
Farm	64217428
Farm Newtake	642753
Higher Plantation	639744
Moor	655744
Plantation	633739
Pound	646746
Pound Farm	64507461
Dunnagoat Cottage	55988648
Dunsford	813892
Wood	795889
Dunstone	71707585
Dunstone	55226425

Dunstone Bridge 71787578
    Brook 552638
    X 71677585
    Down 708760
    Ford 55106429

Dunstone Manor 71657582
Durance 54716571
Dury Brook 663782
    Farm 66187789

E

Eagle Rock 72457230
Eagle Rock 61868870
Eagle Rock (see Looka Tor)
Easdon Combe 683728
    Cot 68287330
    Down 7382
    Farm 72758185
    Hill 733823
    Tor 72958230
East Ash 68009210
    Ash Cross 67989124
    Ash Manor 67959112
    Birch Tor 68908085
    Birch Tor Mine 689809
    Bovey (see Curlicombe Brook)
    Bowden 60359310
    Bowden Wood 60759308
    Brook Mine .... (?)
    Cleave Wood 507845
    Combe 53218860
    Combe 68418712
    Combe 74898500
    Combe Cottage (see Easdon Cot)
    Combeshead 64265841
    Dart Hotel 64917899
    Dart River 608855
    Down 78239110
    Down 604942
    Down 775800
    Fingle 74359141
    Glaze Brook 660618
    Hill 596938
    Horridge 76157422
    Horridge Gate 76137423
    Hughes Mine 592699
    Lake 61199479
    Lodge 73897876
    Lounston 78627510
    Mil Tor (N) 599901
    Mil Tor (S) 599897
        (both mis-spelt Mill on map)
    Mill Tor (see East Mil Tor)
    Nuns Mine 61506993
    Ockment 605880
    Ockment Farm 60509120
    Okement (see East Ockment)
    Park 59049392
    Peeke 68135890
    Rook 60606075
    Rook Gate 60606150
    Shallowford 69417560
    Tor (see Great Trowlesworthy Tor)
    Tor 541899
    Tor 53488996

East Tordown 69729164
    Underdown 71059121
    Vitifer Mine 70868232
    Webburn 708803
    Week 66519194
    Wheal Friendship (see Devon United
                                              Mine)
    Wheal George 529703
    Wheal Robert 51817068
    Wray 78058283
    Wray Cleave 783829
    Wray Quarry 78208313
Easter Green (see Yes Tor Green)
    Head 702632
    Lane Cross 71067510
Eastern Beacon (see Ugborough Beacon)
    Cleave Plantations 790771
    Cleave Wood 508846
    Red Lake (see Outer Red Lake)
    Tor 584665
    Whitaburrow 66536517
    White Barrow (see Eastern Whitaburrow)
    Wood 54127200
Eastlake 61199479
Eastlands Wood 515790
Easton 71958870
    Cross 71908880
Eastontown 53607270
Eastwrey Barton 78108285
Ebworthy 74538152
Eden Farm 72106300
Edward's Path .... 58136719 (S)
Eggworthy 54407190
    Siding .... 549??711? (?)
Eight Stones .... 63??93??
Elbow Gutter .... 58576693 (SE)
    Lane 53646996
    Reave 58506690
Elephant's Nest 51728000
Elford Town 52136741
    Town Farm 52206695
Ellacombe 72338601
Ellensfield 51317623
Ellimore 77718139
Elliots Hill Farm 72427375
Ellisborough House 59846811
Elsford Farm 79258332
    Rock 78628299
Emmet Copse 843814
Emmet's Post 56736314
Emsworthy Gate 74177615
        (Hemsworthy Gate on map)
    Farm 74587655
    Lane .... 74407633 (NE)

Emsworthy Mine	744761
Mine Stream	744761
Rocks	752769
Engine Leat	62987012
Ensworthy Cottage	66198926
Hill (see Quannon)	
Settlement	659889
Ephraim's Pinch	67727853
Erme	638577
Erme	621669
Head	621669
Head Stone	62066728
Islands	636641
Long Row	63506442 (N)
Pits	623668
Pits Ford	62506681
Pits Hill	626669
Plains	640645
(slightly mis-placed on map)	

Erme Pound	63776558
Pound Ford	63756560
Pound Rings	640655
Ermewood	64015739
Essary Bridge (submerged under Burrator Reservoir)	
Farm (see Essworthy)	
Essworthy (submerged under Burrator Res)	
Estrayer Park	570940
Evil Combe	605679
Water	605679
Exeter Inn	75516982
Eylesburrow	59956860
Common	5969
Mine	598682
Mine Road	58086735 (E)
Reave	56096611 (NE)
Smelting House	592677

F

Factory Cross	69418782
Fairbrook	73??83??
Fairhaven	68109215
Fairview	68458849
Fairy Bridge	64167250
Fall Rocks	67996472
Fardel Bridge	61495771
Fat Man's Lane	69496068 (N)
Fatherford Cottages	60509488
Viaduct	60309472
Feather Bed	566682
Tor	535741
Tor	74728155
Featherbed Lane	67168708 (W)
Feathertor Ford	54017410
Fenny Ford (see Venney Ford)	
Fernfires Wood	616616
Fernside	656661
Fernworthy Bridge	662?839?
Circle	65508411
Plantation	6583
Reservoir	666841
Well	662?839?
Fice's Bridge	57777584
Well	57627583
Fieldfare	65946961
Figgie Daniel	73488235
Filfer Head	65946961
Fingle Bridge	74308995
Gorge	741898
Mill	74568975
Fire Stone Cross	66799302
Firestone Ley	668931
First & Last (see Victoria Inn)	
First Crossing-Place	62009145
Firth Bridge	69758088
Fish Combe	564908
Combe Head (see Fishcombe Head)	
Combe Water (see Fishcombe Water)	
Lake	646678
Lake Gully	646678

Fish Lake Marsh	643678
Ponds	751784
Fishcombe Head	565903
Water	572893
(head of stream mis-placed on map)	
Fisherman's Bridge	64757410
Fishes Stones	71398088,
Fishes Stones	72458084,
Fishes Stones	71688101
Fishlake Mires	643680
Fitches' Holt	751?767?
Fitz's Well	59209377
Five Acres	664913
Cross	78207492
Oaks	72806715
Reaves	590662
Wyches Cross	80557830
Flagpole	549?889?
Flat Rock	53507599
Tor	609816
Tor Pen	613816
Tor Water	601807
Flatters	600836
Fleece & Firkin	75716978
Fleetwood Plantation	828828
Flock O' Sheep Rocks	628907
Flour Rocks	68217401
Foale's Arrishes	738759
Foggintor Mire	563739
Quarry	567735
School	56067485
Fold, The	54616927
Footpath Lane	73559158 (NW)
Ford	73218113
Brook	641931
Brook	604630
Farm	64329360
Farms	60756155 & 60996182
Gate	73018086
House	72159190
Mine	64359230

21

Ford Mine Leat	62859231
Newtake	699709
Park	676863
Rocks	60756195
Forder	69616672
Forder	67108969
Forder	80077998
Forder	72248892
Forder	71046102
Bridge	65928983
Brook	651892
Cottages	69997380
Lane	70406045 (NE)
Forderbridge	70027379
Fordgate	73008085
Fordsland Ledge (see Foresland Ledge)	
Fore Hill	621616
Stoke	69827005
Foresland Ledge	576888
Forest Gate	62247858
Inn	65517262
Mine	56??90??
Forstall Cross	52618312
Foster's Pool	72867180
Four Aces	683815
Four Aces	684812
Four Aces	682811
Four Aces	684808
Cross	78467535
Winds	56077487
Fowley Cottage	56509342
Fox and Hounds Cross	52528670
Inn	52538669
Fox Hill Stile	68659011
Fox Inn	53107058
Fox Tor	51387883
Fox Tor	62606980
Cafe	59097350
Combe	630702
Farm	62937055
Farm Ford	62817037
Gert	628697
Gulf	627695
Head	627696
House	62716983
Mires	6170
Newtake	6170
Stream	627695
Foxes' Holt	63999245
Holt	625923
Yard	765815
Foxhole Mine (see Wheal Frederick)	
Foxholes	547852

Foxholes	605785
Water (see Methern Brook)	
Foxhunter, The (now Leg O'Mutton Inn)	
Foxworthy	69427409
Foxworthy	75818210
Bridge	75758206
Mill	75728208
Tor	761821
France Hill	706906
Franklands	83568143
Freeland	756809
French's Lane	69727557 (NE)
Frenchbeare (see Great Frenchbeare)	
Cleave	6784
Gate	67448558
Tor	67158542
Frenchbeer Rock (see Frenchbeare Tor)	
Frenchanger's Corner	73937796
Frenchman's Road	58807332 (NW)
Grave	54508052
Fritz's Grave	73186738
Frog Mill	67959054
Froggymead Circle (see Fernworthy Circle)	
Hill	656841
Rows (see Fernworthy Rows)	
Fuge's Post	57158196
Fullaford	73316588
Pool	73356578
Pool Cross	73396577
Fullamoor	51287169
Corner	51587200
Fur Tor	56557249
Fur Tor etc (see Vur Tor...)	
Furlong	70708970
Furnum Regis	67168129
Fursdon	75218416
Mine (see Ramsley Mine)	
Furze Acres	68496733
Cottage	52737373
Hill	620636
Hill Copper Mine	51856925
Hill Settlement	620636
Park	70798423
Furzehill Wood	517692
Furzeland Down	497707
Mine	49537052
Furzelands	80508630
Furzeleigh	74576774
Furzeleigh	48768114
Cross	81967968
Mill	74516700
Furzemoor	53676521
Furzetor	54337170

G

Gallant le Bower	720701
Gallaven Brook (see Headon River)	
Down	638888
Ford	63508860
Mire	632885
Track	64259008 (SW & NE)
Galler Bottom (see Gawler Bottom)	
Gallows Hill	514851
Gartaven Ford (see Gallaven Ford)	
Garth's House	66946278
Gate Cottage	49917332
Gatehouse Farm	51327766

Gawler Bottom	640784
Lake	637779
Gawler's Hole (see Hollowcombe Bottom)	
George Inn	(?)
Ger Tor	547831
Giant's Basin	59166696
Grave	76768740
Hill	597668
Gib Hill	510684
Gibbet Hill	503811
Pits	502808
Gibby Beam	667677
Combe	686687
Combe Tor	679686
Combe Wood	689687
Gidleigh	67108840
Castle	67158841
Chase	673877
Common	654877
Cross	67248832
Leat	63978801
Mill	67408874
North Park	673877
Park	675879
Park Bridge	67788794
Park Hotel	67708800
Pound	67108849
South Park	673875
Tor	67128779
Gidley's Turn	83968528
Gipsy Corner	79177884
Rock	54??71??
Gingaford	69956233
Cross	70256244
Gisperdown	69936300
Gladstone Rock	80258124
Glasburrow	65986029
Glascombe Ball	659603
Bottom	665607
Corner	66266097
Ford	66226100
Hill	665602
Plantation	665609
Glasscombe etc (see Glascombe)	
Glassy Steps	67088751
Glaze Bridge	67735991
Combe (see Glascombe)	
Brook	660618 & 660614
Head (see East Glaze Brook)	
Meet	66816040
Glazebrook House	69025913
Glebe Farm	66508840
House	58717369
Glebelands	734666
Gledswood House	69098800
Glen, The	71467273
Globe Inn	70098748
Globe Inn	70078750
Gnats Rocks	61646791
Goadstone	55677064
Hill	554704
Pond	55707067

Gobbet Mine	64687280
Plain	645728
Gold Box, The	61807031
Park	702817
Golden Dagger Dry	68288031
Dagger Mine	682804
Fleece (now Highwayman's Inn)	
Lion	75806998
Spout	70037379
Spring	62309185 (?)
Goldsmith's X	61607018
Goodameavy	53186462
Bridge	52906461
Gate	52906461
Goodlay's Plantation	730790
Goodstone Cross	78647202
Woods	785734
Goose, The (see The Grey Goose)	
Goose Eye	74037577
Pool	68307280
Gooseford (see Higher Gooseford)	
Cross	67679184
Mine	676918
Goosepool Copse	68246226
Goosey Creep	519817
Gore Hill	702777
Gorse Pool	65957292
Gorselands	68988420
Gorsemoor House	66309040
Gnatham Barton	52306910
Graddon Cross	56419330
Cradner Rocks	78108025
Grandpa's Grave	60757049
Grange Plantation	623607
Granite Block Works	566737 (?)
Song	70878880
Grant's Pot	62996710
Gratnar	72048349
Gratnor	74207950
Gratton	52706715
Ford Bridge	52936702
Graveyard, The	643916
Graveyards	565876
Gray Weather	70668031
Grea Tor (see Smallacombe Rocks)	
Great Aish	68886025
Bridge	75387026
Cator	68357703
Combe	693694
Combe Tor	523775
Copse	816820
Doccombe	77748683
Dunstone	71547555
Ensworthy	66038949
Frenchbeare	67508580
Gnats Head	616977
Hill (obliterated by Cholwichtown Clay Works)	
Hound Tor	743790
Houndtor	74927953
King Tor (see King's Tor)	
Kneeset	589859

Great Links Tor	552867
Lot Wood	718726
Lounston	78457508
Marsh	541817
Mire Stream	627850
(Manga Brook on map)	
Mis Tor	562769
Noddon	53908740
Parford	72828846
Rock	82168182
Sloncombe Farm	73648618
Sortridge Mine	50907235
Staple Tor (see Great Steeple Tor)	
Steeple Tor	542760
Stone	67157475
Stone Park	671748
Tree Farm	70539038
Trowlesworthy Tor	580643
Varracombe	628842
Weeke	71458760
Weeke Mine	71258747
Western Reave	563720 (N & S)
Wheal Eleanor	733832
Wood	715721
Greatastones	71538843
Greatcombe	69496911
Greathill Copse	791824
Plantation	765922
Greator	75147910
Rocks	747786
Greatrock Copse	824817
Greatweek Cross	71478760
Green Bottom	637751
Bottom	637651
Bridge	82008895
Combe	696835
Down	714696
Dragon Inn (now Swallerton Gate Cottage)	
Gert	554832 (?)
Hill	636678
Hill	568797
Lake	635652
Lane	784771
Lanes	75507280 (NW)
Lanes Gate	78047732
Tor	562864
Tor Water	564864
Greena Ball (see Yearlick Ball)	
Greenacres	69738754
Greenaway	66458818
Greenawell	72988599
Greendown	70716613
Greenhill	63459442
Copper Mine	627934
Copper Mine Leat	62??93??

Greenhill Micas	64956556
Greenwell	52668448
Brook	539656
X	54256564
Down	539659
Down Gate	53776573
Greenwell Farm	53446598
Gert	540657
Greep Quarry	53178892
Gregory's Arms (now Globe Inn, Chagford)	
Gren Tor (see Grenny Tor)	
Grendon	49527807
Bottom Gate	68217864
Bridge	68807851
Common	6878
Cot	68597852
Farm	68527808
Strips	67857770
(Contd NW, NE, SW)	
Top Gate	67847855
Grenny Tor	55108798
Grenofen	495715
Bridge	49007098
Hill	496710
House	49387110
Grey Goose	69416434
Goose's Nest	74037577
Mare (mis-named)	73547302
Wether	71157868
Wethers	60757763
Wethers	63898313
Wethers Stream	638834
Greyhills	565640
Greyhound Inn (now Postbridge Garage)	
Marsh	648791
Greypark Wood	723724
Greystone	74959155
Cross	74919152
Greystone, The (see Grey Wether)	
Gribblesdown	683607
Gate	68366087
Grims Grave	61236640
Lake	704811
Lake Mire	704811
Grimspound	701809
Grimstone & Sortridge Leat	55307731
Head Weir	55307731
Manor	51557048
Mines (see East and West Wheals Robert)	
Grippers Hill	685655
Pound	68206478
Gunnery Lodge	58759330
Gut, The	74246721
Gutter Mire	582668
Tor	578669

H

Halesbury	73987838 (?)
Half Bridge	50177669
Moon (now George Inn) Ring	67156300
Half-Way House	73028735
Halford	81177442
Hall Cross	62475982
Farm	50528320
Farm	53297248
Farm	63105970
Lane	53569030 (E)
Lane Bridge	53619021
Lane Gate	53699020
Plantation	634599
Tor (see Tristis Rock)	
Hall's Pit (see Petre's Pits)	
Halls Cleave	777892
Halsanger Common	7474
Cross	75817308
Manor	75807331
Wood	762736
Halstock Bridge	59949363
Chapel (see Chapel Lands)	
Cleave	604939
Corner	60389255
Down	605938
Farm (see Lower Halstock)	
Mine	60789410
Pound	60359306
Wood	607935
Woods Gate	60199376 (?)
Ham Hill	737739
Hameldown	7078
Beacon	70817890
Beech Hedge	70807890 (SW)
X	70418010
Old House	71457865
Tor	703806
Hamilton Beacon	70817890
Hamlyn's House (see Asacombe House)	
Leat	66407115
Newtake	5483
Newtake (see Broadun Enclosure)	
Hamlyns	649785
Hammerslake	77438170
Hand Hill	6169
X	61306930
Hanger	61385868
Down	6258
Down Clump	62175852
Down Cottages	61295887
Hangershell Rock (see Hangershiel Rock)	
Hangershiel Rock	65505935
Hangerwell	67???3??
Stream	673733
Hanging Stone	58506365
Hanging Stone	56577817
Hanging Stone	55127629
Hanging Stone	55607769
Hanging Stone	61608620

Hangingstone Hill	617861
Hangman's Hole	672715
Hollow	672715
Pit	67297150
Hannaford Copse	777742
Farm	70607073
Manor	70717090
Stickles	703705
Hannicombe Wood	735896
Happy Valley	675805
Hapstead Camphill	71896688
Ford	67066923
Harbourne	695651
Ford	71796231
Man	69646505
Wood	720618
Harbourneford	71706225
Cross	71336188
Hardridge Wood	720723
Hare Tor	551842
Hare Tor	557805 (?)
Harefoot Cross etc (see Haresfoot...)	
Harepath	67219282
Harepath	71759220
Haresfoot Cross	73707662
Mires	739766
Harford	63805950
Ash Farm	63835940
Bridge	50597675
Bridge	63635956
Bridge Farm	50487686
Bridge Gate	63605957
Moor	647625
Moorgate	64325954
Harlyn	67319280
Harragrove	51907697
Harrowbeer	513684
Aerodrome	517675
Harrowthorn Gate	62506160
Plantation	622619
Hart Hole Lane	67137319 (NW)
Tor	581720
Tor	60109112
Tor Brook	593723
Tor Marsh	592720
Tor Rifle Range	581722
Harte Gate	56326542 (?)
Harter Hill (see Hartor Hill)	
Hartland (see Hartyland)	
Moor	6480
Tor	64177992
Harton Chest	76728172
X	77258227
Down	7682
Hartor Bottom	581725
Corner	60209194
Farm	60509120
Ford (see Higher Hartor Ford)	
Ford	60049190
Hill	602918

25

Hartor Hill	603677
Hole	604920
Newtake	603915
Hartyland	64487950
Harvey's Newtake	527817
Harwood Plantation	507697
Hatchwell Corner	70517760
Farm	70217750
Hatherleigh	79608066
Copse	798806
Hawkes Well	74327654
Hawkeswell	74047644
Hawkmoor Cottages	80238055
Mine	798818
Shining Ore Mine (see Hawkmoor Mine)	
Hawks Hollow	561893
Tor	55226252
Hawns & Dendles	6162
Gorge	618623
Hawson	70936842
Court	71696812
Cross	71046819
X	71046819
Hawthorn Clitter	633862
Hay Wood	542669
Haydon Boundstone	63108799
Hayford	68796710
Leat	66726677
Haylake	78069220
Hayne	74808057
Hayne	76288522
Brook	730802
Cross	75068069
Down	7480
Rocks	742804
Haytor Consols	745761
Rocks (see Hey Tor and Low Man)	
Vale	770771
Haytown	52257055
Hazel Tor (see Ausewell Rocks)	
Hazelwood	83038040
Headborough	74997030
Headland Bridge	69298114
Mine	69328098
Warren	6881
Warren Farm	69328110
Headlands	51517628
Headless X	77118783
Headon Hill	631880
River	632885
(mis-named Gallaven Brook on map)	
Headweir Cottage (submerged under Burrator Reservoir)	
Ford	62267099
Garden	58556620
Heap O'Sinners	66206690
Hearn Firs	600743
Heath Close	683815
Cottage	81748820
Stone	67128373
Wood	816880

Heather Knoll	602941
Stone	72107940
Heathercombe (see Hethercombe)	
Heathery Dell	618667
Heathfield Cross	59926016
Down	602601
Park	52756849
Heatree Common	724802
Cross	72988097
Down	724802
House	72708070
Leat	71708026
Heavens Gate	77728086
Hecklake	53627309
Heckland	81938490
Heckwood	54127325
Plantation	543736
Quarry	54497380
Steps	54387297
Tor	53907374
Tor Quarry	53887371
Hedge Barton	73287895
Down	736783
Hedgemoor	80708580
Plantation	810860
Heidi's X	58307042
Hel Tor (see Heltor Rock)	
Hele	72098418
Cross	74527040
Cross	61306103
Cross	71998473
X	72128415
Plantation	482696
Heltor Rock	79968702
View	80358675
Hembury Barn	72516897
Castle	726684
Plantation	732688
Woods	728686
Hemstone Bottom	648834
Rocks	646835
Hemsworthy Gate (see Emsworthy or White Gate)	
Mine	74407610
Rocks (see Emsworthy Rocks)	
Hen Tor	59336530
Henchertraw	669627
Heng Lake	651671
Gully	653671
Henlake Down	633572
Hennaford Stone	72007660
Hennafoot Stone	72007660
Hennock	831809
Henroost (see Hensroost)	
Henry's Ford	60629101
Hensroost, The	652711
(mis-spelt on map)	
Hensroost Bridge	65507099
Gully	654702
Henscott Path	51528350 (S)
Plantation	512832
Hentor Brook (name misplaced on map)	589657

Hentor Cooler	59016560
Cot	58996555
Hill	5965
House	59016560
Meadow	587657
Warren	5965
Herne Hole	581746
Herring's Knock	70857815
Hethercombe	71858105
Brake	717814
Newtake	715809
Hew Down (see Wood Down)	
Lake (see Wood Lake or Wood Hole Stream)	
Hewston Park	720804
Hewstone Gate	72068025
Hexton Plains	585637
Tor	583638
Hexworthy Bridge	65897289
Gate	65137259
Mine	665708
Stream	653726
Hey Tor	75807690
Bound	55188457
Ponds	76027748
Quarries	760774
Heytor Down	7677
Granite Tramway	7577
Heytree Down etc (see Heatree…)	
Hickaton Circles	676659
Hill	6766
Hickley Plain	665623
Ridge	673624
High Down	52208466
Down	530854
Down Clam	53198570
Down Ford	53198570
Down Gate	52328469
Down Steps	53198570
Moorland Visitor Centre	59017349
Tor	51207869
Willes	580894
(mis-spelt Willhays on map)	
Willhays (see High Willes)	
Highbury	71298862
Bridge	67808850
Higher Badworthy	68086171
Beara	71176169
Beardon	51828421
Belliver	53206551
Binnamore	68636140
Blackabroom	52808700
Bonehill	72607750
Bottom	655665
Bowden	81818060
Bowden	55809179
Bowdley	74587224
Bridge	51567762
Brimley	79607671
Brownswell	76307200
Butterbury	54997938
Cherry Brook Bridge	63407699

Higher Collaton	51507526
Combe	77528252
Combe X	77768252
Coombe	69996810
Corndon	69148521
Corner Pool	71537109
Creason	52508066
Crossing-Place	64759058
Dittisham	53557049
Down	67516310
Downstow	69556245
Drewston	72588734
Dunnagoat Tor	55738650
Dunstone	71427573
Eggbeer	76809262
Elsford	79258333
Fingle	74419215
Ford (see Red Lake Higher Ford)	
Ford	65756290
Godsworthy	53017727
Gooseford	67709191
Grenofen	49607105
Halstock	60549275
Hartor Ford	58407181
Hartor Tor	59966774
Hazeldon Bridge	49497623
Hisley	78078057
Hole	81608513
Horselake	71998655
Huntingdon Corner	66456802
Hurston	68588415
Hurston	68658416
Jurston	69708451
Knowle Wood	792808
Lodge	72067310
Lovaton	54636611
Lowton	80778752
Lowton Down	813871
Luckdon	74498286
Lutton	69696122
Meavy Bridge	54606699
Meripit	65347960
Mill	51557763
Moor Plantation	771907
Murchington	68608849
Natsworthy (see Natsworthy Manor)	
Parford	71418995
Pennington	50607211
Piles	646618
Piles Ford	64376172
Pizwell	66817848
Plantation	741729
Plantation	826836
Plantation	627608
Plantation	741729
Plantation	675880
Plantation	517810
Prewley Moor (see Sourton Common)	
Priestacott	61809455
Pudsham	71817432
Quarry	52207385
Shapley	68318472

Higher Shilstone	66029008
Sigford	78167440
Spring	49658023
Statsford	50747265
Stiniel	70628553
Stonelands	81498049
Swincombe	63937255
Terrace	(?)
Thynacombe Woods	706635
Tor	69797260
Tor	61289171
Town	734663
Uppacott	70127288
Watern Farm	58827498
Weddicott	70108600
Whiddon	76287260
White Tor	620786
Whitehill Brake	764919
Willowray	77508349
Willsworthy	53598167
Withecombe	69838928
Woolholes	683640
Highgrove	74157112
Highhouse Corner	60516295
Ford	60516295
Newtake (see Highhouse Waste)	
Waste	609628
Highland	50167152
Highwayman Inn	53489033
Hill Bridge	53208038
Bridge Leat	53138036
Copse	840843
Cottages	56607370
Farm	70266787
Farm	83608425
Farm	80957390
Farm Cottages	75458755
Head	682784 (?)
Hill's Pit (see Petre's Pits)	
Hillbridge Consols	53408075
Hillcrest	83528470
Hillside	70206049
Hillson's Brake	605613
House	63676229
Hilltown	53508100
Wood	541722
Hillyfield Plantation	71906220
Hingston Down	770859
Hill	588694
Rocks	769858
Hisley Wood	779803
Hitchcombe Wood	770897
Hoax Tor (misnomer)	
Hobajohn's X (see Hobajon's X)	
Hobajon's X	65506048
Hobb's Nose	68076371
Hobhouse	69809210
Hockinston Marsh	695718
Tor	69517194
Hockmoor	728675
Head	72766733
Plantation	730677

Holcombe	75108680
Holditch	50888005
Enclosures	562674
Mine	509801 (?)
Hole Farm	68528612
Rock	75677850
Stone	75617849
Holeland	79209057
Holetown	53957260
Wood	543728
Holewell Farm	54107116
Holland Barn	67479340
Villa	50697278
Hollow Combe	623793
Bottom (see Hollowcombe Bottom)	
Hollow Tor	73137620
Hollow Tor	57107454
Holloway's Field	62189249
Hollowcombe Bottom	623793
Holmbush Waste	589618
Holming Beam (see Omen Beam)	
Holne	706695
Brake	787793
Bridge	73017059
Chase	7271
Chase Castle	724719
Chase Hotel	72167092
Chase Mine	72317148
Gate	69737000
Lee	684699
Mill	71336850
Moor	6770
Moor Leat (see Hamlyn's Leat)	
Moor Mine	675698
Park	725704
Ridge	667700
Town Gutter	67787023
Turn	74717050
Turn	71857080
Well	67906870
Wood	701704
Holnepark Cottages	72996995
Holt, The	77328491
Holwell	50057312
Bridge	73937796
Brook	734778
Down	738775
Farm	74337740
Ford	74??????
Lawn	744782
Lawn Cot	74347794
Manor	74487740
Mine	746774
Rocks	739776
Tor	751777
Holy Brook	680687
Brook Bridge	70236877
Brook X (see Hawson X)	
Street (see Holystreet)	
Street Wood	688879
Trinity Church	67078838

Holy Trinity Church	74236659
Trinity Church	73629085
Holyeat	47207992
Holystreet Manor	68908780
Homefield Farm	65859315
Homelands	77427261
Homer Hill (see Brent Fore Hill)	
Red Lake	566819
Homerton Brook (see Fishcombe Water)	
Hill	562905
Mine (submerged under Meldon Reservoir)	
Honeybag Tor	729787
Honeyford	74959180
Honeypool Bridge	65918980
Corner	65878965
Mire	658897
Honeywell	77587568
Hoo Meavy	52766575
Bridge	52616567
Farm	52926609
Hook-in-the-Tor (see Hucken Tor)	
Hook Lake	645649
Hookner Down	7081
Farm	71488249
Tor	699813
Hookney Tor etc (see Hookner...)	
Hooks Bridge	77777366
Cottage	78847332
Cross	77907261
Farm	77607361
Plantation	776729
Hooper's Gert	607?683?
Valley	607683
Hooten Wheals	665708
Hore Wood	749895
Horn Hill	552705
Horn's X	66927110
Hill	679712
Horndon	521801
Bridge	52297950
Down	526812
Lane	52127995 (S)
Hornet's Castle	67967488
Horra Burrow	74947700
Horrabridge	5169
Horrabridge	51316991
Horridge Common	755750
Copse	768737
Horse Brook	711615
Ford	66307112
Ford X	66017134
Hole	601801
Horsehill	73727025
Horsepit X	74328470
Horseshoe Bend	62009145
Falls	71067042
Horsey Park	5878
Horsey Park	580813
Horseyeat	54527025
Horsham	75708144
Bay	75398169
Horsham Cleave	760816
Steps	75938170
Horton's Combe	626666
Hortonsford Bottom	628662
Brook	622658
Hospit Cross (see Bovey Cross)	
X	74328470
Hound Tor (Manaton) (see Great Hound Tor)	
Hound Tor (Walla Brook) (see Round Tor)	
Houndtor Circle	74107877
Combe	752788
Down	743786
Inn (now Swallerton Gate Cottage)	
Medieval Village	746788
Ridge	776803
Wood	770805
Hound's Pool	71816469
Houndle Hill	612582
Houndsmoor Wood	762895
Hourden Plantation	737835
Howton Cross	74428705
Farm	74388709
Huccaby	661729
Bridge	65897289
Cleave	659726
Cottage	66117354
Farm	66297310
House	66007280
Ring	65857380
Tor	65667397
Tor Gate	66057405
Hucken Tor	549738
Gate	54797380
Huckworthy Bridge	53147053
Common	532710
Lodge	52937074
Mill	53247042
Mill Meadow	53247042
Mine	53207080
Huggaton Court	602868
Cut	603869 (W)
Pool	60328688
Hugh Down (see Wood Down)	
Lake (see Wood Lake or Wood Hole Stream)	
Stone (see Wood Stone)	
Hughslade Farm	56059310
Humphrey's Cross	72156932
Hundred Acre Plantation	719898
Hunnavil's Bed (see Fishlake Mire)	
Hunt Tor	55708749
Hunter's Path	73618996 (W)
Path	69606129 (W)
Stone	68116314
Tor	76028248
Tor	72208975
Hunting Gate	73608997
Huntingdon Barrow	66206690
Bridge	66716706
Clapper	65706619
Corner	66456615
X	66456619

29

Huntingdon Ford	66486617
Gate	66466619
Hill	661670
Mine	669670
Mine Leat	65396716
Warren	670660
Warren House	66516694
Huntingpark Wood	769839
Hurdle Pool	64007380
Hurston (see Lower and Higher Hurston)	
Castle	68378340
Pound	678829

Hurston Ridge	672826
Water	677818
Hut, The	54358784
Hut, The	68508270
Hutchinson Memorial	59906990
Hux Lake	636672
Ford	63396640
Huxton	54746300
Corner	54986298 (?)
Hyner	83898202
Bottom	832818
Bridge	83688168

I

Ian Mercer inscription	67896865
Ilsington	785761
Common (see Haytor Down and Bagtor Down)	
Wood	791762
Ingo Brake	512846
Plantation	514845
Ingra Tor	555721
Halt	55617220
Inn Down	828844
Inner Dinger	587891
Moor	601660
Pupers	678674
Stal Moor	6362
Inter Moor	601660
Irishmen's Wall	61009200 (E)
House	62129210

Iron Bridge	53846719
Bridge	57307139
Cage Gate	50658090 (?)
Catch Gate	54478949
Gate	48688022 (?)
Gates	54478949
Mills	80688845
Isaford	72427920
Island of Rocks	55829021
Isle of Mona	60507529
Itifer Bottom	685649
Ivybridge Lane	59057348 (S)
Ivy Tor	62809361
Mine	62709340
Water	630932
(name mis-placed on map)	
Ivychurch	67107290

J

Jack-in-the-Box	68236452
Jackman's Bottom	593863
Jacques' Plantation (see Dunnabridge Lower Plantation)	
Jan Reynolds' Cards (see Four Aces)	
Jay's Grave	73227991
Jervis Farm	77289249
Jew Stone	59898273
Jimmie Pickles' Lane	53287039 (SE)
Joan Ford's Newtake	630720
Jobbers	560674
Ford	59156741
Jockey Down's House	54389128 (?)
Joey's Lane	56036808 (SW)
Gate	56036808
John Bishop's House	64117258
Cann's Rocks	814798
Stone	77947749
Johnson's Cut	611813 (E)
Cutting	572737
Jolly Lane	65537263 (ENE)
Cot	65617270

Jonas Coaker, grave of	71897679
Jordan	70097505
Ball	697753
Barn	70087503
Cross	70857512
Lane	517704
Mill	69987505
Jubilee Plantation	746716
Stone, Belstone	62019360
Stone, Leusdon	70757315
Judge's Chair	64617456
Corner	62457610 (?)
Table	642?743?
Jump Gate	50496342
Jurston	69618447
Bridge	69788500
Common	7084
Cross (see Yellands Cross ??)	
Down	6983
Ford	69718434
Gate	69398383
Valley	696835

K

Keaglesborough	571701
Mine	571701
Keble Martin's Chapel	66606660
Kelly	79208183
Cross	79058192
Mine	795818
Kelly's Corner	59359271
Kendon Bog	717820
Farm	71718180
Stream	712818
Kennel Field	58496621
Kennel Field	56706476
Plantation	616598
Kennick	79908400
Reservoir	804844
Kenning Borough	64528890
Kennon Hill	642893
Mires (see Whitmoor Marsh)	
Reave	643885
Kent Tor	51747935
Kerbeam (see Curbeam)	
Kes Tor	66558628
Kestor Inn	75698072
Rock	66558628
Kilmantain	50696942
Kiln Brake	783775
Down	823841
King Down	708812
Lane	55019073 (N)
Tor	709816
Tor Halt	56517320
Wall	53018630 (NW)
Way	53018630 (NW)
King-de-Stone	67??83??
King's Barn	63005940
Barrow	70928144
Bridge	76008567
Gutter	63155922
Oven	674814
Oven Bungalow	67548106
Tor	556739
Wood	63405930
Wood	7166
Wood Mine	711665
Kingford Farm	50357521
Kinghurst	71407024
Down	715705
Down Wood	716707
Kings Arms	(?)
Kings Arms	(?)
Kings Cross	80448001
Kingsett Bridge	57796980

Kingsett Down	5181
Farm	51268036
Farm	57666993
Ford	57796980
Gert	57466991
Kingshead	72827230
Corner	70957695
Farm	71207759
Gate	70967759
Lane	71227761 (W)
Tor	70887812
Kingswell Newtake	735752
Kiss-in-the-Ring	63506442
Kit Hill	615824
Mine	56296745
Rocks	61308270
Steps	61188220
Kit's Stone	67716712
Kitts Bridge	52068444
Cottage	51958458
Mine	51728450
Steps	51728454
Kitty Tor	56728747
Klondyke	59309400
Corner	59409398
Knack	608882
Ford	61458858
Mine	614884
Knackersmill Gulf	632663
Knatta Barrow	65986420
Knattaborough	61099100
Knattaburrow Hill	658643
Pond	65606448
Knattleborough (see Ryder's Hill)	
Kneeset Foot	57858667
Nose	58748684
Pan	590855
Knock Mine	614884
Knocking Mill Corner	(?)
Combe	624668
Combe	632663
Knoll	56158360
Knowle	53036987
Knowle	78988054
Knowle	74706951
Down	528699
Ford	53086992
Plantation	669580
Wood	533641
Knowles Cross	74736960
Krapps Ring	644781

L

L Corner	72507833
L Stone	72507833
La Wallen Chapel	66948892
Lade Hill	6382
Bottom	638820
Brook	633823
Lade Hill Marsh	636823
Lady Brook	629916
(mis-named Ivy Tor Water on map)	
Modiford's School	53286978
Well	63909411
Lady's Wood	685591

Ladybrook Tor	62549236
Lake	65307730 (?)
Lake	52828889
Lake	53106825
Lake	70437229
Down	540890
Steep	705725
Viaduct	53358890
Weir Stream	679747
Lakehead Hill	644776
Newtake	6477
Lakeland	68358304
Bottom	683832
Lakemoor	69706775
Plantation	696677
Wood	699690
Lambhole Wood	505842
Lambs Down	695662
Farm	69806601
Park	56266763
Waste	695662
Lamerton Lane	605843
Lane End	53708215
Head	53708237
Head	68706900
Head	50477883
Lane's Shaft Gully	689808
Langaford	70886875
Langaford	57408792
Bridge	70198495
Hill	70408450
Hill	707690
Langaller	80657657
Langamarsh Pit	684719
Langawell	68207210
Langcombe Bottom	603670
Brook	617662
Burrows	603671
Hill	6165
Meet	60196719
Langdon	72338280
Bridge	74258100
Lane	74258100 (N)
Lane Gate	74258100
Langey Sands	63907361
Langham Bridge	60815914
Langhill	74608641
Langlake Mires (see Cator Bog)	
Langland Wood	774898
Langmead	79507341
Langridge	640845
(Long Ridge on map)	
Field	645855
Gate	64108431
Langsford	51077676
Langston	67319010
Langstone	55037871
Langstone	74718230
Cross	74278170
Cross	76147093
Hill	744820
Manor	52487379

Langstone Mire	552784
Moor	5578
Moor Circle	55637820
Langworthy	52448538
Bridge	76007370
Brook	755744
Farm	70197710
Hill	707772
Lanson Brook	622721
Lantern Inn	74606980
Laployd Barton	80038591
Down	794867
Plantation	803850
Larkham Wood	703657
Laughter Tor (see Lough Tor)	
Launder	69466976
Lawn, The	55186845
Lawns Corner	52997690
Le Rowe Rewe	67276735 (SE)
Le Rowe Rew	65756170 (NNW)
Lea Side	80808914
Leaman's Mead	678650
Leaning Rock	58506365
Leaping Salmon Inn	51306997
Leapra X (see Liapa X)	
Leather Tor (see Lether Tor)	
Lee Gate	55217188
Leat	58716620
Moor	5964
Leebeer Wood	527651
Leedon Hill	5867
Tor	563719
Leeper X (see Liapa X)	
Leetown	52587072
Wood	523707
Left Lake	648633
Clay Works	647634
Ford	64466358
Micas	64606330
Mires	649633
Leg O'Mutton	51746799
Corner	51776790
Legis Lake	569662
Lake Mires	569662
Tor	57106557
Tor Warren	5765
Leigh	84268097
Leigh	68078777
Bridge	68328764
Cross	84278090
Cross	70506110
Cross	67205742
Cross Hill	703607
Farm	78398760
Gate	66775801
Grange	70796118
Lane	67205742 (NW)
Steps	68328764
Tor	711714
Tor Farm	70907186
Tor Pound	71397131
Leighbeer	52986421

Leighbeer Plantation	527645
Leighon	75557920
Bridge	75407934
Cross	75708017
Tor	759788
Lemon, The	763775
Lemson (see Lambs Down)	
Lenda	79357562
Lane	79397590 (SW)
Wood	790757
Lent Hill	73567041
Lessonpark Copse	776915
Letchole Plantation	758810
Lether Tor	563700
Bridge	56906996
Farm	56706980
Lettaford	70208401
Cross	70998409
Down	698837
Leusdon	70707321
Common	705730
Green	70767318
House	70707320
Lodge	71067315
Lewdons Farm	78078391
Lewdowns Cottages	77708437
Lewthorn Cross	77957610
Ley	50987980
Ley	72307935
Cross	72297948
Ridge	71837092
Liapa	70218332
Bog	700830
Bog Stream	702826
X	70228332
Newtake	700830
Lick, The	538745
Lid Gate (see Lyd Gate)	
Lily Meynell Memorial	68376342
Lime Stream	(?)
Limsboro' Cairn	56588054
Lincombe	69008449
Linhay Hill Quarry	770711
Linscott	73708747
Cottages	74058725
X	74108719
Lints Tor	580875
Brook	583875
Lissicombe Foot	52398428
Head	52378416
Littaford Tors	61577715
Little Aish	69546060
Anthony	65946918
Aune	648692
Bee Tor	61627690 (?)
Belpool Island	69897115
Boulters	52467800
Boy	68347513
Bullhornstone	67806012
Cocks Tor	528765
Combe Tor	52057772
Cross	70566968
Little Crow Tor	60697871
Down	819811
Down Tor	57686937
Ensworthy	66068935
Fox Tor	62156980
Frenchbeare	67538575
Gem Mine	49007080
Gnats Head	60826743
Gnats Head Leat (see Philips Leat)	
Hare Tor	54698413
Hen Tor	59346528
Hill	637877
Hill	606894
Hound Tor (see Little Whit Hill)	
Howton	74458715
John's Walk	81967968
King Tor	552740
Kneeset	586842
Langridge Gate	64178465
Langridge Newtake	645855
Links Tor	54718698
Man	67716712
Mis Tor	56407630
Noddon	532864
Petre	65426559
Pew or Pu Tor (see Sampford Tor)	
Roost	67717520
Round Plantation	54407335
Sherberton	63817349
Sherberton Steps	63907361
Sigford Farm	77797386
Staple Tor (see Little Steeple Tor)	
Steeple Tor	53867537
Thorn	68748623
Tor	590897
Trowlesworthy Tor	57706459
Uppaton	61535790
Varracombe	633837
(mis-placed on map)	
Weeke	71328769
Whit Hill	632899
(Little Hound Tor on map)	
Whit Tor	538787
White Tor (see Little Whit Tor)	
Wonder Bridge	54827419
Wooston	76358862
Littlecombe	70336892
Livaton Cross	67679351
Pits	64559235
Liverton	806752
Brook	777765
Lizwell	70697440
Bridge	71197410
Meet	71337370
Wood	710743
Loampark Cottage	78688239
Locks Gate Cross	69637398
Lodge Wood	799791
Logwell Rock	71047342
London Bridge Corbels	55667335
Inn	51306986
Inn	75556985

London Inn	56855962
Pit	64559235
Long Ash	54777433
Brook (see Pila Brook)	
Clapper (see Little Wonder Bridge)	
Hill	553747
Leat	55047423
Newtake	552744
Pits	557745
Ponds	54997470
Wood	546736
Long Island	69907100
Island	72807171
Island Ford	69907100
Knave	71727851
Lane	54506945 (NW)
Marsh	535831
Newtake	642723
North Wall, The	61538890 (N)
Plantation	595750 (N)
Plantation	551808
Pool	751784
Pool	55468309
Ridge (see Langridge)	
Longaford Newtake	6177
Tor	616779
Long-a-traw	682644
(mis-placed on map)	
Corner	68156468
Island	68106429
Longbetor Newtake	560795
Longbettor	54418017
Longford	51857472
Leat (see Wheal Fortune Leat)	
Longland Barn	75808294
Longstone	66028567
Longstone	65495828
Longstone	65426073
Longstone	55357460
Longstone	55037874
Longstone	73547302
Bottom	661852
Brook	662854
Hill	5691
Lane	55706846 (S)
Leat	59156741 (60156721)
Manor	55686844
Mire (see Langstone Mire)	
Longstone, The	58506365
Longtimber Tor	50947826
Look-and-Weep	80827577
Looka Tor	68507202
Lookout Castle	59807173
Tor	59707233
Loothorn Cross (see Lewthorn Cross)	
Lord Mayor's Castle	56158360
Lough Tor	653757
Loughtor Combe	663757
Gate	65737560
Heath	6575
Hole	663757
Hole Farm	65807592

Loughtor Hole House	66127578
Man	65217538
Newtake	650755
Pound	65267558
Lovaton	54456620
Brook	552654
Ford	54536603
Pit	61619281
Lover's Leap	72677225
Lover's Leap	72657220
Lovey Lee's Snail Farm	60887068
Low Man	75707705
Lower Aish	70617209
Badworthy	68176192
Beara	70996135
Belliver Farm	52906558
Birch Pool	73506807
Birchy Gate	61839297
Blackaton	69487796
Blackaton Cross	69787783
Bonehill	72507742
Bowden	82008021
Bowdley	74647223
Bridge	69626037
Brimley	80107701
Broadun	639801
Brownswell	76357200
Budbrooke	75509210
Butterbury	54797972
Cadworthy Farm	54936433
Cator	68827626
Cherry Brook Bridge	63117481
Cheston	68305835
Collaton	51487520
Corndon	69208530
Corner Pool	71457154
Creason	52518077
Creason (see Creason)	
Crossing Place	65209120
Dittisham	53557067
Down	793783
Down Cross	79907819
Downstow	69616232
Downtown	52208549
Drewston	72488741
Dunnagoat Tor	55758632
Dunstone	71657589
Eggbeer Farm	77149172
Elsford	79118273
Factory Cottages	69758792
Ford (see Red Lake Ford)	
Ford	66806328
Godsworthy	52787761
Goodameavy	52976472
Halstock	60159360
Hannaford	70747051
Harter Tor	60356752
Hartor Ford	57907150
Heltor	79538745
Hole	81508551
Hookner	71518240
Horselake	71998655

Lower Huntingdon Corner	667665
Hurston	68648416
Lake	53226784
Longford	51727453
Lounston	78477500
Lowery Farm	55636923
Lowton	80758760
Lowton Down	813875
Luckdon (see Luckdon)	
Meavy Bridge	53856719
Meripit	65807916
Natsworthy	72257965
Pennington	50527205
Piles	644608
Pizwell	66817845
Priestacott	61959462
Pudsham	71727454
Quarry	51907380
Sanduck	77288280
Shapley	68318478
Shilstone	66109001
Sigford	77807387
Sigford Bridge	77607378
Stiniel	70648550
Swincombe	63957259
Terrace	78527935 (W)
Thynacombe Woods	708628
Tor	69787256
Town	71127290
Town	737662
Town	701729
Town	53048059
Uppacott	70147282
Waye	77207171
Weddicott	70308591
Whiddon	76217254
White Tor	61927922
Whitehill Brake	769913
Willowray	77918304
Withecombe	69708890
Lowerdown Cross	79907818
Lowery Cottage	55636923
Cross	54876920
Crossing	55006923
Farms	55??69??
Stent	55586926 (N)
Tank	55606937
Tor	55606980

Mabor Farm	52486565
Wood	523658
Maggie X	65177921
Magpie Bridge (see Bedford bridge)	
Mill	49927049
Maiden Hill	588795
Tor	56206810
Main Head	662591
Maish Hill	625825
Brook	626821
Gate	62788332
Gate Ford	62788332

Lowton	74318597
Boro'	667835
Brook	668824
Farm	665834
Hill	667835
Mires	668824
Rocks (see Lowton Boro')	
Luckcombe Stone	64906925
Luckdon	74608272
Luckey Tor (see Looka Tor)	
Lud Brook	662592
Gate (see Lyd Gate)	
Gate	76797729
Lug Tor (see Looka Tor)	
Lukesland	64165798
Farm	64115780
Grove (see Lukesland)	
Wood	636581
Lurgecombe	75527127
Mill	75517126
Lustleigh	785813
Cleave	7681
Mill	78548095
Shining Ore Mine (see Kelly Mine)	
Lutton	69556128
Green	696613
Lyd	557884
Gate	68406733
(mis-named Lud on map)	
Gate Stroll	683674
Lydda Bridge	54908819
Lydford	511849
Bridge	50948457
Castle	50928479
Gaol (see Lydford Castle)	
Gorge	506842
Sharp (see Sharp Tor)	
Tor	59957818
Viaduct	51358468
Lydgate House Hotel	65207869
Lydia Bridge	69596068
Mill	69506080
Lyle's Corner	53888820
Lynch Common	5566
Down	5566
Hill	546666
Tor	565807
Lynscott (see Linscott)	

M

Manaton	750812
Gate	74998130
Hill	713807
Rocks	74838156
Mandles	63928486
Lane	63908473 (N)
Manga Brook (see Great Mire Stream)	
Ford (see Mangersford)	
Hill	6385
Hole	64008518
House	63928486
House Lane	63908473 (N)

Manga Rock	63608580
Mangersford	64008603
Manor House Hotel	73158448
Inn (now Burrator Inn)	
Road	695873
Mansel Wood	543729
Mansion, The	59846811
Map Stone	77998181
Mapstone	78218166
Marchant's Bridge (see Higher Meavy Bridge)	
X	54596680
Ford	54506696
Mardle	667692
Bridge	73606625
Combe	669692
Ring	67526868
Mardon Cross	80108395
Down	772879
Maristow Inn (now Burrator Inn)	
Market Hill	52876456 (NW)
Gate	52426474
Marley Farm	72186133
Marntory Rock	65??59??
Marsh, The	662730
Marwood's Cross	67885805
Mary Tavy	503793
Bridge	49887885
Clam	51037845
Inn	50487886
Reservoir	51298163
Mason Gate	53367280 (?)
Master Rock, The	52358065
Mattins Corner	66606660
Maunder's Brake	512812
Maximajor Stone (see Headless X)	
May's Newtake	634705
Corner	63507015
Maynard's Valley	609684
Meacombe Cottages	73088680
Farm	72768677
Meadcote	67109075
Meadhay	81458880
Meadhaydown	802886
Meadow, The	633663
Meadow, The	69258109
Meadows, The	665754
Meads	63705890
Meads, The	568828
Meadstown	73338368
Meavy	541672
Lane	52126780 (SE)
Pool	579661
River (see Mewy)	
Mel Tor etc (see Mil...)	
Meldon	56009238
Common	6986
Copper Mine	569917
Dam	563916
Down	5592
Farm	56199250
Glassworks	567920
Granulite Quarry	566920
Meldon Hall	70008659
Hill	696861
Junction	55659215
Lane	55989241 (NNE)
Pool	564921
Quarries	568925
Reservoir	561912
Viaduct	56509234
Woods	566927
Mere's End	565707
Mire	565707
Meripit Hill	658803
Mine	659792
Merivale	549752
Antiquities	555749
Bridge	55007508
Bridge Mine (see Wheal Fortune)	
Cottages	54807520
Farm	54757509
Quarry	546753
Warren	554753
Merlin's Cave	60527528
Merrifield	67676168
Lane	69459106 (NE)
Plantation	673617
Merrivale (see Merivale)	
Merryfield	73016625
Mether Brook	577917
Metheral Bog	673832
Brook	672830
Farm	67298395
Gate	67038375
Hill	6289
Hole	622892
Marsh	673832
Methern Brook	601791
Hill	601795
Mewy River	584733
Meynell's Bank	655650
Michel Combe	694687
Michelcombe	69656895
Down	6869
Lane	68706900 (E)
Mid Devon Copper Mine	632945
Mid Tors	53466929
Middle Brook	614797
Brook	657638
Brook Ford	66526330
Brook Old Wheelhouse	66216350
Cator	68277675
Combe	77738203
Drewston	72598739
Ford	59859120
Heltor	79458739
Hill	587910
Hill	607880
Hill	590731
Hole	81698534
Meripit	65257950
Mires	635669
Pizwell	66817846
Rook	60326085

Middle Shotts	772774
Staple Tor (see Middle Steeple Tor)	
Steeple Tor	540756
Stoke	69667053
Tor	66908583
Venton	69499103
Week	66369210
Middlecott	71558605
Middlecott	78197695
Wood	782765
Middlemoor	49807290
Middleworth Farm	57206918
Gate	56896930
Lane	56896930 (SE)
Plantation	574689
Tor	57256935
Midlands	51457980
Mil Pool	69107224
Tor	693725
Tor Wood	693723
Milfordleigh Plantation	684878
Mill, The	66187231
Mill Bridge (see Wisdome Bridge)	
Bridge	65779442
Corner	592665
End Hotel	71278927
Farm	74988087
Farm	66119175
Farm	69589249
Hill	669757
Lane	66259191 (SW)
Leat	71336851
Leat	67307535
Park	573701
Park	561645
Pond	51997761
Wood	767757
Millawns	71998371
Millhill Copse	837815
Miltor Lane	69477269 (N)
Valley	692722
Wood	693723
Miller's Mile	68207411
Mine Leat (see Wheal Friendship Leat)	
Miner's Path	68208100 (E)
Mistor Farm	570755
Marsh	569776
Marsh	570752
Marsh Stream	568766
Pan	56307687
Warren	562755
Mistress Piece	719722
Molehills	567917
Money Pit	64506035
Money Pit	68177384
Monkey's Castle	50147342
Monks X (see Pixies' X)	
Path	69596068 (S)
Withecombe	69608932
Monksmoor	67355726
Monkswell	52047109
Farm	52097113
Monkswell House	51867070
Wood	522708
Moon's X	65249411
Cross	65249411
Moor Alders	807887
Barton	81828340
Barton	78578460
Brook	592909
Cottage	58349337
Cross	70406399
Farm	65969116
Gap	52407291
Gate	52498535
Gate	52428532
Gate	70078325
Lodge	60597497
Shop	51347460
Tongue	651725
View	65649225
Wood	778835
Moorgate	67705923
Cottage	59299312
Farm	59609304
Ford	59159313
Moorhaven Hospital	667575
Moorhayes	73917990
Moorland Hotel	76757723
Park	69606057
Moorlands	67745818
Farm	62457351
Moors Head	71286341
Moorshead Brook	713634
Cross	71416310
Moortown	66508912
Bottom	664891
Farm	52637405
Gate	66388915
Leat	66198913
Moorwood Mine	777838
Moreton Inn (now Warren House Inn)	
Moretonhampstead	754861
Moses Bawden's Grave	55637501
Mother Nicholls' Book Place	59016560
Mount Ararat	79807475
Clog	53676323
Flaggon	69388894
Misery	634705
Misery X	63637058
Pleasant Cottages	56607475
Mountsland	75927398
Common	754744
Copse	759741
Moute's Inn	61778527
Moyle's Gate	73897990
Mrs. Bray's Wash-hand Basin	55797525
Mucks Hole Bridge	64877945
Gate	65187951
Muddilakes	612757
Newtake	6275
Muddy Lakes (see Muddilakes)	
Brook	612758
Leat	62407484

Mullicroft Cottage ....552?686?
     Farm .... 552?685?

N

Nakers Hill 646685
    (name mis-placed on map)
    Pits 639696
Nancy's Castle 67158130
Nap 694699
Narracombe 78707676
    Wood.................................. 789765
Narracott 75659155
Narramore 75718440
Narrator Brook .... (592692)
     Farm 56656880
Narrow Tor 56716870
Narrow Combe (see Narracombe)
Nat Tor 57356730
Nat Tor 54588239
Nattadon 70598698
    Common................................... 705866
Natsworthy Ford .... 72078020 (?)
    Gate 72108020
    Hill 714800
    Manor 72117998
    Plain 719800
Nattor Down.. 543827
    Farm 57156729
    Farm 54158228
Natty's Castle 67158130
Neadon 82618720
Neadon 75058248
    Cleave...................................... 758818
Needle Buttress................................... 53886380
Nelder's Lane .... 55826775 (NNE)
Netherton House 73549109
Nettlery ....63008759 (E) (?)
Netton 82268221
    Cleave Wood 823820
New Birch Tor & Vitifer Consols (see Birch Tor
          & Vitifer Mine)
    Bridge 71137089
    Bridge 59619031
    Bridge 75648001
    Bridge (see Drakeford Bridge)
    Barn 75498340
    Barn 62105990
    Engine Leat 60606778
    Forest Corner................ 56587640
    Forest Enclosures 5876
    Forest Gate 57587679
    House (now Warren House Inn)
    House.............................. 74007555
    Houses 81818693
    Inn (now Northmore Arms)
    Inn (now Warren House Inn)
    Inn (now Leaping Salmon)
    Inn (now Drewe Arms)
    Inn (now Elephant's Nest)
    London 59357375
    Take................................... 688745
    Warren (see Legis Tor Warren)

Murchington 68758830
Muswell 72837230

New Warren Tor (see Legis Tor)
    Waste 627611
    Waste Gate 62586142
Newbridge Common 7071
    Hill 710712
    Hill Corner 70807118
    Hill Cottage 70807107
    Marsh 710708
Newhouse Ford 73967573
Newlands Brake 668606
Newleycombe Bottom 594700
    X 59167029
    Farm 58746995
    Gert 59357020
    Gert Stream 594701
    Lake 599707
    Mine 586699
    Mine Ford 58456983
Newpark Farm 55306608
    Waste 596612
    Wood 595608
Newton Barton 71209219
Nine Maidens 61239283
    Stones 61239283
    Stones 66136916
    Stones 65259223
Ninney Lake 569806
Nipper's Hole 580795
Nodden Gate etc (see Noddon...)
Noddon Ford 53258630
    Gate 53008631
    Quarry 53398666
    Steps 53258630
Norsworthy Bridge 56786939
    Farm 56836945
    Lane .... 57837006 (W)
    Plantation 568697
North Betsy 51208226
    Bovey 740839
    Bovey Bridge 73778371
    Bovey Common 7182
    Bovey Cross (see Bovey Cross)
    Brentor (see Brentor)
    Creber................................ 66008798
    Devon United Mine (see Devon United
               Mine)
    Devon Wharf 52026773
    Gate 54427080
    Harton 76678280
    Harton Down 764829
    Hele 61406120
    Hessary 5774
    Hessary Tor 57837422
    Hill 67708749
    Hill Lane.....................68268763 (SW)
    Kingwell 76908655
    Lodge 76627872
    Lodge 83808335

North Moor Lane ....62598670 (E)
   Park Wood................................... 727704
   Plantation 597733
   Road .... 58?68?
   Teign 614840
   Tor 69107192
   Walla Brook (see Bovey River)
   West Passage .... 603823 (NW)
   Wharf... 51726511
   Wheal Friendship (see Wheal Betsy)
   Wheal Robert 51207080
   Wood 734678
   Wood 547640
   Wood... 718733
Northcombe 80648030
          Copse 807806
Northdown 68558919
Northmoor 75628824

Northmore Arms 67408968
Northmore's X 61306900
Northpark Copse 77209190
Northway 72307680
   Bridge 72077683
Northwood 82968607
Nuns X 60466991
   Cross Brook 609695
   Cross Farm 60606982
   Cross Ford 60866975
   Cross Hill 604699
   Cross Mine 599698
Nurston 71906400
Nutcracker Rock 74357529
Nutcrackers 77248141
Nutley Cottage 50987530
   Farm 50977561

O

O'Brook, The 647703
Oak and the Ash, The 62258135
Oak Coppices 779779
   Hill 69706070
Oaken Combe 679749
Oakery, The (see The Ockery)
Oakery Bridge (see Ockery bridge)
Oakhill Cross 69686068
Oakley Cottage 52617320
   Farm 52257340
Oakmoor... 715736
Ochre Works 516781
Ock Tor 612900
        (mis-spelt Oke on map)
Ockerton Court 602868
Ockery, The 59517420
Ockery Bridge 59507419
   Hill 594740
Ockment Hill 6087
      (mis-spelt Okement on map)
Ockside Hill 6187
Oke Brook (see O'Brook)
   Tor (see Ock Tor)
Okehampton Camp 588930
       Castle 58359425
       Chase 5892
       Common 5790
       Golf Course 578939
       Moor Gate 59159312
       Park 585937
       Trust Stone................. 52252468
Okel Tor (see Hucken Tor)
Okement Hill (see Ockment Hill)
Old Bottle Inn (now Fleece & Firkin)
   Cleave Wood 502436
   Farm 60166990
   Hay (see Jobbers)
   Hill 667629
   Hill Rocks 66826310
   House 71457865
   House Hill 7178

Old Inn 71797675
   Jack 76887809
   Mill Bungalow 77238997
   Mill Leat.................................... 76998995
   Mill Leat 69008781
   Police Station Cafe 58927355
   Rectory Farm 61159375
   Summer House, The .... 74???3??
   Town Hill................................... 788760
   Walls 67608664
   William 77127790
Oldcleave Wood................................. 503838
Olde Yarde 73328373
Older Bottom 598704
   Bridge 59827054
Olderdown Shotts 779773
Olderwood 52406647
   Plantation 528667
Olditch Farm 64589345
Oldsbrim etc (see Ollsbroom...)
Ollsbrim etc (see Ollsbroom...)
Ollsbroom 68827343
   X 68557348
   Newtake 688733
   Plains 687734
Omen Beam 588772
   Bottom 593777
   Farm .... 58???7??
   Tramway   57857500 (N & SE)
One Mill Bridge 76258544
   Stone Bridge 52668177
OP 15 60258778
Orchard Pool 74206706
Osborne 74198620
Otter Pool 66557258
Ottery Tor (misnomer)
Outcombe Brook 579679
   Corner 58336830
   Farm 58036851
   Ford 58076856
   Gate 57786829

Outcombe Rocks	57796844
Waste	578686
Outer Dinger	580883
Huccaby Ring	655744
Newtake Plantation	664742
Pupers	67186740
Red Lake	571820
Stal Moor	6265
Standon (see Knoll)	
U Stone	64306640
Ovals Tor	751777
Over Brent	69606203
Tor	558753
Tor Gert	560755
Overbrent (see Over Brent)	
Wood	688618
Owlacombe	787780
Beams	767735
Bridge	77147360
Owlacombe Burrow	77647763
Cross	76497276
Farm	76637315
Mine	772735
Owley	67615971
Bottom	680595
Bridge	67735995
Corner	67005975
Lane	67075980 (E)
Leat	66465986
Mill	67695995
Moorgate	67075980
Oxen Tor (see Cadworthy Tor) (??)	
Oxenham	77607372
Arms	65109353
Cross	66289442
X	66289442
Manor	66519423

P

Pack Horse Inn	(?)
Packhorse Road	53777008 (NW) (?)
Packsaddle Bridge	78918024
Padley Common	698870
Paisley Mead	51557649
Pale Farm	83088533
Pall Brook (see Piall Brook)	
Palmer's Newtake (see Hamlyn Newtake)	
Palstone	70526004
Pan Pool	71286468 (?)
Parford	71308990
Parford	72688872
Well	71258968
Wood	71309020
Park Cottage	72317941
Cottage Inn	55906792
Gate	55916798
Gate	79169091
Wood	712719
Parkland	59246192
Parklands Farm	71366709
Parktown	54717323
Parlby Arms	53107058
Parliament Rock	61537573
Parnell's Hill	690650
Parson White's Babeny	673757
Parson's Brown Loaf	77998181
Cottage	61507557
Field	520655
Wood	545668
Parsonage Wood	501835
Pascoe's Cottage	580?750?
Well	58077500
Payne's Bridge	65809158
Peak Hill	556699
Plantation	552694
Pear Tree Cross	75046932
Peas Corner	53398168
Peat Cot	60557151
Farm	60507140
Peat Cot Hill	607712
Peathy's Path	686643
Peck Farm	75978281
Pits	764832
Peek Hill	556699
Moor Gate	67725930
Peekhill	54586980
Plantation	552694
Pen Beacon	599629
Moor	6063
Moor Reave	60026281 (E)
Ridge	6064
Shiel (see Shiel Top)	
Pencleave Wood	577943
Pendennis Copse	72606460
Penlee Farm	65537873
Penn Beacon etc	(see Pen...)
Wood	805746
Pennaton	68615949
Bridge	68435929
Pennpark	78287254
Plantation	784725
Pennsland Bridge	74977250
Lane	75427265 (W)
Pennycomequick	51557401
Penstave Copse	690613
Pepper Lane	68827579 (E)
Pepperdon Down	778851
Farm	77508515
Peregrine Fur Farm	771893
Perry Memorial	64808508
Perryman's Bridge	78057738
Peter Cross Tor (See Western Whitaburrow)	
Peter Tavy	514776
Brook	552782
Combe	522777
Cross	50817649
Inn	51247776
Mill	51507758
Peat Track	53007805 (E)

Petertavy Great Common	5578
Wood	509774
Pethybridge	78008100
Petre-on-the-Mount	65986905
Petre's Bound Stone	65976905
X	65356548
Pits	659648
Pits Bottom	658637
Pits Pool (see Knattaburrow Pool)	
Pew Tor	533735
Common	5373
Sett	533735
Pewtor Cottage	53357326
Phillip's Leat	60586770
Phillpott's Cave	63016720
Piall Bridge	59616043
Brook	585606
(headwaters just off Dartmoor)	
Picket Rock	53987619
Piddledown Common	730900
Pig Lane	66988654 (E)
Piggie Rock	72958228
Pig's House	64247190
Pigs Leg Cross	52848911
Pigshill Droke	66908580
Pikedstone	68477601
Pikedstone	67987666
Pil Tor	73507595
Pila Brook	572751
Piles Brook	649612
Copse	644621
Corner	64756214
Gate	64906125
Hill	653609
Newtake	646617
Valley	643620
Wood	644621
Piley Brook (see Piall Brook)	
Pilgrim Farm	78448727
Pinchaford	76897663
Ball	762765
Pinckes Lake	56686427
Pinmoor	75938872
Pinswell	585783
(name mis-placed on map)	
Cut	591841 (N)
Ford	59308452
Hill (see Little Kneeset)	
Pipe Track	53356358 (E)
Piper's Beam	659660
Pit	72098019
Pithill Farm	63355775
Wood	636578
Pitt Farm	75407070
Parks Bridge	72107779 (?)
Pitton	72157868
Brake	719790
Pittpark	72227830
Pitts	720801 (?)
Cleave Quarry	502762
Cottage	56086762
Pixey Close	81308040

Pixeycombe	54166757
Pixie Glen	507844
Pixies' Cave	56506811
Cave	667?729?
X	50137366
Holt	66507255
Holt	67057329
House (see Pixies' Cave)	
House	69456805
Parlour	720?896?
Pits	767769 (?)
Pool	58488950
Rings	674614
Wood	667729
Pizwell	66817845
Bottom	670783
Bridge	67007763
Cottage	67017765
Ford	66977850
Green	669786
Steps	66967850
Place	76487120
Cross	76147093
Wood	76257140
Wood Camp	76197138
Plague Market (see Potato Market)	
Plaister Common (see Plaster Down)	
Consols	50907235
Plaistow Green	802868
Plantation, The	682615
Plaster Down	5172
Plaston Green	79788685
Play Cross	70586930
Plum-Pudding Hill (see Great Noddon)	
Plume of Feathers Inn	59067341
Plumley	80058013
Plym Consols	586699
Ford	61056850
River	621683
Steps	60206720
Plymouth Inn	75208603
Leat	(55096801)
Points	54558875
Poldice Mine	49407054
Polford Bridge	76119271
Ponsworthy	70187406
Blacksmith's Shop	69987380
Bridge	70117389
House	70187405
Mill	70107384
Pook's Cottages	82228620
Pool Down Wood	798757
Farm	79877541
Poole	81708603
Pork Hill	518749
Portland Lane	558673
Lane Bridge	55936760
Villa	77907580
Post Inn	(?)
Postbridge	649789
Postbridge	64827891
Postman's Road	64557468 (NE)

Postman's Path .... 72527750 (W)
Pot Hole 74266691
Potato Market 554750
Potter's Way ....67279427 (NE) (?)
Pound Rock 73978415
Poundsgate..................................... 70607210
Powder Mills 628774
    Cottages...................... 62807692
    Farm 62807692
    Leat 63908131
Prayley Mead .... (?)
Prescombe 51508407
    Corner 52198343
Preston 75009039
Prestonbury Castle 747900
    Common........................... 747902
Prewley Farm 54849110
    Gate 54699097
    Moor 543907
Priestaford...................................... 74606864
    House 74126879
Primm Cottage 69547349
Prince Albert 77847749
    Arthur Consols (see Wheal Betsy)
    Edward Bridge 60797501
    Hall 62577420
    Hall Avenue ....62427468 (S)
    Hall Bridge 62607386
    Hall Newtake 630743
    Hall Plain 619748
    Hall Rocks 61397407
    of Wales........................ 76007839
    of Wales Inn 58907353

Quannon 648899
Quarry Ford 64269007
    Lane .... 52677385 (W)
    Pit Plantations 645577
    Track 58487336
Quarrymen's Path .... 53057710 (SE)
Queen Victoria's X 65617262
    of the Dart Mine 735688
"Queen of the Moor" (see Vur Tor)

R.A.F. 29 Sqn Memorial 71218071
Rabbits Holt 641924
    Tor 63386998
Raddick Gate 57807048
    Hill 577712
    Lane .... 57807048 (SW)
    Plantation 5770
Raddon 50618493
    Wood 507844
Radge 50617640
Rails 64008603
Railway Inn (now Devil's Elbow)
Railway Inn (now Fleece & Firkin)
Rajah Brooke, Tomb of 56036763
Ram's Parlour 71017146

Princetown 5873
    Prison (see Dartmoor Prison)
Princep's Folly 67118779
Prison (see Dartmoor Prison)
    Leat 57487950
    Quarry 581745
Pritton's Works................................69757102
Proctor's Gully 640888
Prospect Lane .... 64829322 (E)
    Place..............................64829322
Providence Place 67508928
Prowse's Crossing 54906831
    Rock 64835730
Prowtytown....................................52607439
    Brake 528745
    Lane .... 53057451 (W)
    Rocks 52857452
Pu Tor (see Pew Tor)
Puckie Stone 68378762
Puddicombe House 72599205
Pudhanger (see Moorgate Farm)
Pudsham Down 730748
    Down Gate 72227445
    Wood 713739
Pullabrook Farm 79257952
    Wood 786698
Puggie Stone 68378762
Pullaford (see Pullabrook Farm)
Pulpit, The 57656399
Pupers Hill 6767
    Rock 67296738
Purps Farm 54076247
Putty Moor 546819

Q

Queenie Meads............................... 629916
    Pool 66707280
Quick Bridge 59136078
Quickbeam Foot 6464
    Hill 656647
Quicksilver's Grave ....674?618?
Quintatown 70398642
Quinter's Man 621839
Quintin's Man (see Quinter's Man)

R

Ramshorn Down 793739
Ramsley 65309320
    Farm 65329297
    Hill 65109300
    Mine 65109310
Ranny Brook (see Renny Brook)
Raspberry Garden 62428605
Rattle Brook 559869
Rattlebrook Hill 5585
    Hill 555871
    Mine 559857
    Peat Works 55998709
    Railway 5488
Raven Butress 53886380
    Rock 73017156

Raven Rock	71207147
Rock	68507202
Raven's Tor	76148190
Raven's Tor	50418400
Raybarrow Pool	638900
Rectory Lane	54146762 (S)
Wood	737904
Red Barrows	67707964
Brook	656631
Brook Ball	660632
Brook Higher Ford	65756290
Brook Lower Ford	66956273
Brook Middle Ford	66586254
Brook Mires	657630
Cottages	566737
Lake	646666
Lake Clay Works	645668
Lake Combe	566828
Lake Ford	63696622
Lake Hill	5781
Lake Higher Ford	64236641
Lake Lower Ford	63696622
Lake Rushes	638664
Lion	(?)
Red-a-ven Brook	585895
Dip	584907
Gulf	628616
Lake	629617
Linhay	62566135
Reddacleave	70026394
Brakes	698644
Kiln Cross	70416394
Reddaford	53708334
Leat (see Wheal Friendship Leat)	
Newtake (see Hamlyn's Newtake)	
Water Junction	78857899
Reddapitt Lane	62385987 (W)
Reddicliffe Farm	51807288
Head	(?)
Redford (see Raddaford)	
Leat (see Wheal Friendship Leat)	
Newtake (see Hamlyn's Newtake)	
Redlake Farm	70439240
Redoubt Pits	596897
Redstone	55??68??
Redwater Bridge	68208099
Brook	681814
Reed	83538380
Rendle Stone (see Rundlestone)	
Renny Brook	625633
(mis-spelt Ranny on map)	
Rent Stone, The	71677585
Resugga	61799295
Rew	75447075
Cross	75507076
Mine	75417062
Rewdown Cross	75077110
Rewe Lake	640886
Rewlea Cross	75507103
Rex Bridge	68458008
Ricketts Hill	691711
Riddipit Farm	56997007

Riddipit Gate	57377002
Gert	57137006
Lane	56947000 (E)
Steps	56906996
Stream	573701
Riddon	67607636
Bottom	673767
Brake	66907773
Down	670762
Gate	67627641
Ridge	6676
Ridge Lea	68308376 (?)
Ridgeon's Leap	55587210
Ridgey Cross	71206926
Ridgnor	74128349
Right of Way	53908155
Riland Plantation	515714
Ring Hill	648793
O'Bells	52148286
O'Bells	70038751
of Bells	74068390
of Stones	55637820
Rock	57??86??
Rock	58098176
Ringhill	64657940
Coppice	672941
Copse	64727931
Cross	67209416
X (see Ringhole X)	
Newtake	648793
Ringhole X	67159417
Ringleshutes Gert	675697
Mine	67627009
Mine Road	69737000 (W)
Ringmoor Circle	56106590
Cot	55846660
Down	5666
Rings, The (see Ryder's Rings)	
Ripman's Gate	73207350
Rippator (see Ripper or Rival Tor)	
Ripper Tor	64318802
Rippon Tor	747756
Rifle Range	751736
Rising Sun	65059361
Rit Lane	67187516 (S)
Wells	669748
Rithy Pits	607907
Rival Tor	64318802
River Dart Country Park	732703
Robert's Brake	603605
Roborough Down	5165
Hill	757704
Rock	51556714
Umber Works (see Ashburton Umber Mine)	
Rock Copse	816803
House	81808778
Inn	52186781
Inn	77127720
Plantation	544725
Rockleaze	53416892
Rockpark Cross	76507089

Rocks, The	568833
Rockside	64929285
Rogues Roost	52307381 (?)
Rogues Roost	67787507
Roman Altar	70138751
Bridge	51908448
Chair	60509408
Mine	688809
Roman's X (see Blackaton X)	
Rook Lane	60836005 (N)
Lane End	60836005
Reave	60006183 (N)
Tor	60256168
Wood	599613
Roos Tor	543766
Bottom	540772
Pits	537766
Sett	543766
Rora Down	797745
House	80157437
Wood	801749
Rosalie	60??63??
Rough Tor	60607981
Rough Tor	57906850
Rough Tor (see Row Tor)	59309164
Marsh (see Rowter Marsh)	
Moor (see Rowter Moor)	
Plantation	574686
Roughtor Combe	598913
Combe Stone	59859120
Ridge	594907
Ridge Stone	59709078
Round Cross	73706682
Field	54??81??
Hill	611744
Hill	575667
Hill	649855
Hill	694832
Hill	704814
Hill	575648
Hill Farm (see Roundhill Farm)	
House	77918303
O Plantation	833822
Of Beef	75748206
Plantation	77918303
Plantation (see Hanger Down Clump)	
Pound	66398684
Tor	62898901
Wood	557806
Wood Gate	55178039
Rounders Hole	667694
Rounders Hole	66496924
Roundhill	78209199
Farm	60647423
House	60567467
Stream	607745
Tor	60547393
Roundy Farm (see Roundpark Farm)	
Hill	579703
Park	63957965
Pound	65829028
Pound	66398684
Roundypark Farm	57807011
Routrundle Farm	55407170
Gate	55507160
Lane	55217189 (SE)
Leat	57017297
Row Brook	683728
Tor	59309164
Tor	60607981
Tor Brook (see Rowter or Middle Brook)	
Tor Combe (see Roughtor Combe)	
Tor Marsh (see Rowter Marsh)	
Tor Ridge (see Roughtor Ridge)	
Tor Wall	62067970 (NE)
Rowbrook Farm	68407250
House	68707249
Rowden	69997638
Rowden	49457555
Ball	69897599
Brook	(?)
Cross	70157632
Down	699760
Rock	81218601
Tor	699760
Wood	496758
Rowell Cross	51308510
Rowse's Mine (see Wheal Prosper)	
Rowter Brook	614797
Gate	62908027 (?)
Marsh	614794
Moor	6179
Wall	62067970 (NE)
Rowtor (see Row Tor)	
Royal	683835
Gate	68208366
Hill	617726
Oak	54176720
Oak	75616991
Oak	81208920
Oak	69836020
Oak Siding	566737 (?)
Standard	50247982
Tor	61807263
Rubble Heap	75587730
Ruddycleave	72997415
Bridge	73487462
Leat	73527486
Water	(735746)
Rudge	78338080
Wood	783799
Rue Lake	628729
Rue Lake (see Rewe Lake)	
Deep Ford	63037332
Pits	639887
Ruelake Gate	62797359
Rugglestone Rock	72357641
Inn	72057651
Rundlestone	57607497
Corner	57607497
Mission	56717502
Tor	576745
Runnage	66817911
Bottom	669789

Runnage Bridge 66847890
         Circle 67517870
         Ford 66907910
Rush Bottom 594839
         Ford 59118370
Rushford Barton 70808912
         Bridge 70508820
         Manor Pound .... 693?889?
         Mill 70608841
         Mill Farm 70608841
         Tower 70268905
         Wood 703896

Rushlade 75407265
         Bridge 74477380
         Common 743737
Rutt Farm 64805680
         House 64705675
Ryders Ford 67996489
         Hill 660690
         Mire 654676
         Mire Stream 654676
         Plain 678644
         Rings 679644
         Rocks 677647

S

St. Andrew 65309449
St. Andrew 75528609
St. Andrew 75516976
St. Edward 54296310
St. John 51236968
St. John 70947320
St. John 73948381
St. John 78508128
St. Mary 70576950
St. Mary 61929350
St. Mary 50927876
St. Mary 53417247
St. Michael 78527615
St. Michael 60435939
St. Michael 70138750
St. Michael 47088040
St. Michael & All Angels 58687371
St. Pancras 71887680
St. Patrick 69616028
St. Patrick 63825949
St. Paul 52096773
St. Peter 51327779
St. Peter 72047313
St. Peter 54046722
St. Petrock 50908473
St. Thomas 53609030
St. Winnifred 74948129

(The above are all Churches)

St. Gabriel's Chapel 65207920
St. Gudula's X 75316936
St. John's 68968885
St. Leonard's Well 56076760
St. Mary's Abbey 741673
St. Michael's Bungalow 59019362
St. Olave's 68668823
St. Raphael's Chapel 66297302
St. Thomas Cleave Wood 789884
Saddle Bridge 66447191
         Bridge Gate 66457191
         Clove Rock 73207827
         Rock 54107441
         Tor 751763
Saddlesborough 558623
Saint Hill Farm 73228701
Salters Pool 71067061
Sam Parr's House 62497118

Sam's Newtake 636752
Sammy Arnold's Lane .... 60808892 (W)
         Thompson's Cottage 64766592
Sampford Barton 52807143
         Manor 53297248
         Spiney 53507245
         Tor 532731
Sanctuary, The 782763
Sand Path .... 62178545 (S)
         Parks 624704
         Pit 61609280
Sandeman Bridge 65728366
Sanders 70208405
Sandhill Cross 74458704
Sandpit Lane .... 65869120 (W)
Sands Gate Cross 69799023
Sanduck 76848364
         Cross 76638354
         X 76828360
         Grove 774827
         Wood 773835
Sandy Ford 65808950
Sandy Ford 64837112
Sandy Ford 57408792
Sandy Ford 57148336
Sandy Ford 57407922
         Gate 69906460
         Hole Pass 621815
         Hole Plain 624812
         Lane .... 69906460 (SE)
         Meadow 75018081
         Park 71208960
         Park 684812
         Park Bridge (see Dogamarsh Bridge)
         Park Inn 71188960
         Park Mill (now Mill End Hotel)
         Path .... 58056659 (N)
         Pit Gate 74197403
         Pool 64007380
         Road .... 65808950 (SW)
         Road .... 63508860 (SE)
         Way .... 68706900 (NW)
Sandyways Cross 72038830
Saracen's Head (now Two Bridges Hotel)
Sawdye's Newtake 643757
Saxon Farm 58289333
         Gate 58279334
         Gate Bungalow 58289334

Saxon Gate Chapel	58219323
Scab Bottom	683647
Scad, The	569847
Brook	664599
Scae Wood	692679
Scarey Tor (see Skurry or Skir Tor)	
Scatter Rock Quarry	821855
School House, The	65397421
Scobetor	72457500
Rocks	72347500
Scobitor (see Scobetor)	
Scorhill Circle	65488739
Down	658875
Farm	66158765
Gorge	660869
House	66218736
Lane	66118771 (S)
Rocks	65858710
Tor	65858710
Scorriton	704685
X (see Hawson X)	
Down	687683
Gate	68926809
Point	67926870
Scotch Sheepfold	64488090
Scotley Bridge	77729007
Scout Hut	58096731
Scudely Bogs	687787
Scudley Beam	692802
Scum Pool	63957370
Scutely Bogs	687787
Scutley Beam	692802
Seale's Stoke	69407090
Seaman's Borough	766899
Second Crossing-Place	61769095
Sentry Corner	64699180
Set Tor	54??78??
Setters	53277798
Rocks	53277798
Seven Lords' Lands	74127622
Sisters	67227441
Star Gate	52998160
Stars	65339448
Seventeen Brothers	61239283
Shaden Brake	548633
Moor	547636
Plantation	546638 (?)
Shady Combe	535656
Shadyback Tor	56666506
Shallow Ford	57317820
Shanty, The	69656975
Shaptor	81318072
Down	810810
Rock	80958085
Shapley	71488299
Common	697826
Cross	68278509
Tor	669821
Sharp Tor (Double Dart)	686730
(Erme)	649417
(Lustleigh) (see Sharpitor)	
(Mewy) (see Sharpitor)	
Sharp Tor (Tavy Cleave)	55358321
(Tavy)	52547710
(Teign)	729899
(Wallabrook)	55018488
(E. Webburn)	72867806
Sharpitor	560703
Sharpitor	77228142
Sharra Marsh	698716
Pool	69717163
Pool Marsh (see Sharra Marsh)	
Shaugh Beacon	537636
Bridge	53276368
X	54456309
Hill	535634
Moor	5764
Moor	559621
Prior	542631
Sharrah Pool etc (see Sharra...)	
Shavercombe Brook	603653
Down	592662
Falls	59516600
Head	608650
Hill	593662
Pound	59366629
Tor	59406618
Shearaback Tor (see Shadyback Tor)	
Sheep Path (see Quarrymen's Path)	
Sheepfold, The	64488090
Sheepfold Corner	623709
Sheeps Tor	566682
Warren	566680
Sheepstor	559676
Bridge	55936760
Brook	582669
Dam	557679
Mine (see Kit Mine)	
Shell Top (see Shiel Top)	
Shelly	65409332
Shelstone Tor	55798980
Sheraleers Wood	598603
Sherberton	64607336
Bridge	64687313
Circle	63947318
Clam	64767371
Common	6973
Firs	648736
Great Newtake	635730
Steps	64767371
Shere Wood	736686
Sherraback Tor (see Shadyback Tor)	
Sherrell (see Sherwell)	
Sherrill (see Sherwell)	
Sherrill (see Sherwill)	
Sherwell	67957489
X	68357386
Sherwill Farm	62075770
Cottage	62225744
Wood	618576
Shewte	79317916
Cross	79547890
Rights	78967815
Shiel Top	59826382

Shiel Top Brook	582642
Top Reave	59826382 (S)
Shilla Park	550760
Pool	65209120
Shillapark	55007591
Shilley Pool (see Shilla Pool)	
Shilstone	70209070
Combe	657898
Gate	66009017
Hill	658902
Leat	65608986
Tor	65829020
Venn	700910
Shiny Pool	(?)
Shipley Bridge	68096288
China Clay Works	67956288
Cottage	68206288
Gorge	682632
Leat	66806392
Naptha Works	67956288
Pool	68086280
Tor	68516319
Shipping	82908680
Sholedon	694700
Shortacombe	52808700
Lane	53008631 (NW)
Shorter X	71378643
Shorts Down	502725
Shortsland	49757279
Shot Plantation (see The Shotts)	
Shotts, The	774772
Shotts Bottom Wood	774771
Shovel Down	657858
Down Antiquities	660859
Stone	73307632
Shuggle Down (see Shovel Down)	
Shute Cross	68065827
Down Coppice	732905
Gate	67505842
Lake	671835
Lake	677786
Shuttaford	71806916
Shuttamoor	82158295
Siddaford Tor	633830
Sig	758763
Gorge	767744
Sigford	77687389
Bridge	77827397
Consols (see Stormsdown Mine)	
Cottages	77667513
Cross	77687525
House	77737399
Silent Whistle, The (now Fleece & Firkin)	
Silk House	70909178
Silk House	65918345
Silver Brook Mine	78827586
Hill Mine	(?)
Spout	699?739?
Wood	792759
Simms Hill	785757
Simon's Lake	688733
Single Burrow	70557951

Singmoor Cross	71928551
Sittaford Tor (see Siddaford Tor)	
Sitting-Down End	67896865
Siward's X	60466991
Skaigh	63109390
Bridge	63129380
Corner	63389334
Warren	634935
Wood	639939
Skat Tor	82??85??
Skatter Rock	82??85??
Skaur Ford	65027131
Gut	647706
Hill	650703
Skerraton	70086462
Down	703650
Gate	70086502
Skir Gut etc (see Skaur...)	
Ford	60829293
Tor	60669230
Skit Bottom	607913
Bridge	52068444
Lane	52028460 (W)
Mine	51538460
Mine	607915
Skit's Hole	517844
Skitscombe Wood	669602
Skurry Tor	60669230
Skylark Inn	52136557
Slade	661722
Slade	79958121
Slade	541774
Bottom	539771
Copse	796813
Cross	79908121
Mead	80887690
White (see White's Slade)	
Slade's Well	72807840
Slipper Stones	605924
Slipper Stones	562889
Sloncombe	73628615
Small Brook	685649
Small Brook	627892
Brook Ford	62509062
Brook Plains	686649
Ridge	78128849
Smallacombe	77637690
Smallacombe	554668
Bottom	492793
Cutting	777766
Lake	558666
Mine	777766
Rock	54118681
Rocks	754783
Stream	549872
Water	713813
Wood	55456715
Smallake	80678949
Smalland	50358431
Wood	505842
Smallbrook Plains	686649
Smeardon Down	522780

Smearn Down	522780
Smethaford Island	67337462
Smith Hill	632758
Brook	629762
Farm	63307530
Smith's Wood	773750
Cottage	77307480
Mine	773748
Smithacott	79808490
Smithy Mead	69317930
Smokey Cross	77237629
Smuggler's Hole (see Downing's House)	
Snaily's House	66117625
Steps	66017629
Snakey Island	64737430
Pool	64727427
Snap	528819
Lane	52998160 (SE)
Lane Gate	53108151
Snappers Tor	57106925
Snelling's Copse	830816
Snider Park Plantation	663737
Sniper's Gully	570912
Stream	571902
Snotters Bottom	746778
Snowdon	668684
Brook	673681
Hole	67306810
Soldier's Pond	58707323
Somerswood	69526060
Sortridge Consols Mine	510707
Manor	50617105
Sounscombe Brook	523435
Foot	51988380
Head	52208362
Sourton	53509032
Common	5489
Ice Works	546900
Tors	542899
Soussons	68407902
Common	673787
Down	6779
Newtake	6779
Plantation	6779
Warren	680792
Warren House	68??79??
South Betsy Mine	510810
Brent	698602
Brentor	47908019
Common	558806
Common Plantation	557806
Creber	66078793
Devon United Mine (see Devon United Mine)	
Devon United Mine (see Brookwood Mine)	
Ditch	51807780
Down	556912
Gate	51??84??
Harton	76798212
Hele	61256094
Hessary House	59597316

South Hessary Tor	59707233
Hill	679860 (?)
Hill	781821 (?)
Kingwell	77018622
Lake Farm	53797316
Leigh Farm	80878871
Lounston	78457508
Plain Wood Mine	(?)
Plantation	600726
Tavy Head (see Tavy)	
Tawton	653944
Tawton Common	6390
Teign	640824
Tor	69177161
Zeal	650935
Southbrook	72507295
Southcombe	71377641
Gate	71077646
Hill	713765
Well	71077640 (?)
Southcott	75058024
Down	744801
Rocks	744801
Southerly	52628821
Down	5387
Down Gate	53128800
Southill Leat	67708703
Southpark Wood	731695
Southway	72407665
Southwood	83418610
Sowtontown	51397626
Snider Park Plantation	663737
Spader's Cottage	61507557
Spanish Lake	592642
Spara Bridge	84358409
Sparkatown Farm	53586850
Sparnam Hill	750699 (?)
Spicers Well (see Fitz's Well)	
Spinsters' Rock	70109080
Sptichwick Common	6875
Farm	70907192
Higher Lodge	70557253
Lower Lodge	71587170
Manor	70827258
Meet	71907192
Splash, The	70007379
Splatton Hill	696610
Spriddle Combe	577798
Lake	588803
Spring Rock	54478949
Tide	582642
Spurrell's X	65895995
Square Bookhams	78769055
Pound	655886
Pound	665868
Seat	49??73??
Stable Door Inn (now George Inn)	
Stacombe	77358735
Stacombe's Telling Place	66907110
Staddicombe	72556939
Staddon	67966119
Plantation	683615

Stal Moor	6264
Staldon	6362
Barrow	636623
Reave	62826209
Stall Moor (see Stal Moor)	
Stalldon (see Staldon)	
Stalldown (see Staldon)	
Stamping Mill Leat	60606778
Stamps Gate	61287101
Standon Down	5581
Farm	54508148
Hill	556815
Houses	550825
Steps	53918155
Stanlake (see Stenlake Farm)	
Plantation	568705
Stannary Parliament	61567577
Stannon Bottom	651805
Brook	649816
Cottage	65028064
Great Newtake	6482
Hill	646812
Lodge	65187921
Tor	64658112
Staple Tors (see Little, Middle and Great Steeple Tors)	
Stascombe Telling Place (see Stacombe's...)	
Stats Bridge	66728052
Brook	662807
House	62168247
House Cut	619823 (E)
House Hill	620825
(mis-named Winney's Down on map)	
Stawell's Bush Cross	76817093
Stean Lake	568713
Steart Ridge	637607
Steeperton	618888
Brook	616869
Gorge	618894
Hill	618888
Tor	618888
Tor Mine	614884
Steeple Tors Sett	545755
Sten Lake (see Stean Lake)	
Stenga Tor	56808800
Stenlake Down	568714
Farm	56987093
Stennats	650736
(mis-spelt Stennents on map)	
Stennents (see Stennats)	
Stenteford Bridge	65439380
Stentiford's X	74237604
Stephen's Grave	53627813
Steps Bridge	80468830
Mill	80688845
Steward Farm	76438522
Mill	76508525
Wood	771850
Sticklepath	642941
Sticklepath	49007099 (S)
Bridge	64349401
Bridge (see Bedford Bridge)	
Sticklepath Wood	492706
Stidson	71656030
Stidwell	73537293
Still Pool	64537904
Stingers Hill	633661
Stinhall	70678543
Stiniel Cross	70798553
Stinka Tor	56808800
Stinnons Brook	620776
Hill	6277
Newtake	6278
Stippadon	70886219
Stittleford's X	74237604
Stock Lane	69407020 (N)
Stockey Furzen	679880
Stockman's Newtake	65??75??
Stoke Farms (see West, Seale's, Fore & Middle Stoke)	
Stone	61415940
Stone	82748615
Clay	714745
Copse	711902
Cross	70749101
Cross	71957454
Farm	72097468
Farm	70919082
Ford	60039192
Heath	684631
Hollow	683635
Plantation	618594
Tor	64858568
Wood	615592
Stonelands	81238007
Waste	817801
Stoneslade Tor	712779
Stonetor Bottom	647858
Brook	645854
Gate	65018528
Hill	649855
Marsh	645855
Newtake	6485
Stoney X	55226345
Post	71757021
Stoneycroft	53657220
Stony Bottom	643650
X	55226348
Gert	65556640
Hole	629669
Marsh	691722
Stoodley	71786975
Stooky Moor	5679
Stormdown	77157272
Mine	770728
Stourtown	53207760
Stouters Corner	57219182
Stouts Cottages	72197796
Stowford	64075707
Bridge	64105679
Cleave	637574
Straight Mile	69527943 (SW)
Strane	611723
Ford (see Headweir Ford)	

Strane Hill 6271
    Tor .... 61??71??
Strawbushes Quarry 768711
Stream Hill... 6269
Stream Hill 623716
    Ford (see Headweir Ford)
Strole 68906735
Stubley Hills Gert 53358449
Stumble Corner 69487268
Stumley Corner (see Stumble Corner)
Stumpy X (see Horsepit X)
    Oak 71046819
    Oak X (see Hawson X)
    Post 63379334
"Submarine, The" (see Eastern Whitaburrow)
Sullets Lane .... 66667890 (S)
Summer Brook 600800
    Hill 596806
    House, The .... 751?738?
    Lane................................... 68356022 (N)
Summerhill 74476930
    Cross 74446961
    Farm 58827500
Summerswood Bridge 69306036
Sun Inn .... (?)
Sunny Corner 60877062
    Mount 49707472
Sunnyfield.. 73188726
Sunnyside Cottages 62837709
Sunshine Valley 635696
    (mis-named Swincombe on map)

T Gert 623699
T Gert 662679
    Stream 662680
    Stream 623697
Table Stone 62476680
Tadpole Pond 51707825
Take Off Stone 51848432
Tannaford (see Tunnaford)
Tanners's Path..................... 64806810 (SSE)
Tapter 73607624
Target Railway 58409106
Tavistock Inn 70497210
    Inn (now Church House Inn)
    Inn (Now Cornwood Inn)
Taviton 5007445
Tavy River 595820
    Cleave 555831
    Cleave Plains 554836
    Cleave Tors 555834
    Hole 580820
        (name mis-placed on map)
    Hole Stone 57658258
    House 50418021
    Sharp (see Sharp Tor, Tavy Cleave)
Taw River 609859
    Ford 62009142
    Ford 60938722
    Marsh 620905
    Marsh Reave .... 62749170 (S)
    Plain 620908

Swallerton Gate 73917911
    Cottage 73897915
Swallever Lane .... 54747434 (W)
Swallow Ford 54697441
Swallow Ford .... 69727881 (?)
Swan Inn (now Union Inn)
Swanaford 82108841
Sweaton Farm 70067366
    Lane ....69997308 (NW)
    Plantation 705734
Swett's Wood 618610
Swell Tor 56207320
Swelltor Quarries 560733
Swincombe 639698
    (name of head mis-placed on map)
    Bog 622721
    Cottage (see Dolly Treble's House)
    Farm (see Higher Swincombe)
    Ford 64167250
    Gate 63487357
    Newtake 636730
    Meet 64797371
    Point 64247189
    Reservoir 632718
    Steps 64167249
Swincombe Vale Mine (see Gobbett Mine)
Swine Down 737796
    Gate (see Swallerton Gate)
Symon's Ditch 59309290

T

Taw Rocks 611876
Tawcroft.. 62169281
Tawton Common 6885
    Gate 67928490
    Mill 65819443
Teign Head (see North Teign)
    Marsh 70908831
    View 70508812
    Village 838810
Teigncombe... 672871
    Cleve 66978681
    Common 666868
    Common Lane ...... 67138707 (W)
    Down 666868
    Gate 66698720
    Manor... 67218715
Teignever.. 653871
    Bridge 65468706
Teignhead Clapper........................... 63928448
    Farm 63528432
    Great Mire 628848
    Great Newtake 6284
    Road .... 63??64??
Teignworthy...................................... 67648564
Temperance Hotel (now East Dart Hotel)
Templer's Newtake (see Broadun Enclosure)
    Stone 76357803
Ten-Acre Trees 62007403
Ten Commandments Stones 73507309
Tennacord 77928236

Tennets	689652
Ter Hill	643745
Xs	64137063 & 64217070
Terrace Walk	75407022 (NE)
Thickstone Lake	570644
Thomas Cleeve Wood	789882
Thorn	68309022
Thorn	72558535
Thorn	68488659
Thorn	79688730
Thornhill Lane	73077759 (NW)
Thorns Cross	73038542
Thornworthy	67038490
Bottom	671852
Brook	669856
Corner	66128541
Down	665847
Gate	66998472
Farm	67038490
Pound	67018473
Tor	665851
Three Barrows	653626
Barrows Reave	65756170 (NNW)
Boys	66038549
Brothers (submerged below Avon Reservoir)	
Burrows	653626
Corners	79917890
Crowns Inn	70058749
Gates	77189275
Parish Stone	76347831
Rocks	73217350
Stickles	642739
Throwleigh	668908
Common	6590
Cross	66879075
X	66879075
Mine	672925
Thrushelcombe	590671
Brook	596678
Thule	66598871
Thurlestone, The	62908684
Thynacombe Barn	70506310
Tiger's Marsh	557884
Timber Bridge	65366699
Bridge	57427960
Pool	65207362
Tim's Bridge	65878294
Tin Copse	79628184
Mines	729658
Pits	710787
Pits	52358225
Tinker's Bridge	63906292
Grove Plantation	773921
Tinhill Copse	797820
Tinner's Mill	51496962
Tipleyhill Cross	79987571
Lane	79987571 (NW)
Tipson Gate	66378797
Toad Rock	75748206 (?)
Tolchmoor Bridge	57906185
Tolmen Stone	65508708
Tom's Brake	721622
Hill	647834
Lane	67??74??
Plain	638628
Tongue End	62319490
Top Tor	73607624
Tor Dene	69518736
Down	612943
Down	69499164
Gate	59507327
Gutter	59156741
Hill	735766
Lane	56206759 (NE)
Park	69656095
Rocks	64105912
Rocks Quarry	64115905
Royal	60007312
Royal Newtake	6172
Town (see Tortown)	
View	68749211
Wood	537891
Tordean	72806292
Tordown Corner	52407528
Torgate House	59607341
Torhill	68709044
Torhill	68749049
Torhill	70809221
Farm	74108150
Torland Wood	497742
Torlands Barn	63475880
Torns	74937118
Torpeek Cross	66045660
Torr	61686052
Cott	63925909
Fields	56306792
Torrs Wood	673578
Torry Brook	578625
Tors, The	(?)
Tors End	61449270
Park	61519388
Tortown	51907577
Torwood Copper Mine	537891
Tottiford	81498238
Copse	813822
House	80808229
Reservoir	810833
Tower Hill	762713
Town Barton	74988087
Orchard Rock	78348126
Wood	715731
Wood	785818
Townsend Cross	64829378
Tradesmans Arms	70416864
Trafalgar House	64589383
Traveller's Ford	59157860
Treeland	67806130
Down	673612
Plantation	677613
Treetops	76167985
Trena Bridge	59507420
Trenchford Stream	783851
Trendlebere Down	7779

Trennaway Cross	72759085
Triangle, The	549900
Trips	74768698
Tristis Rock	63836014
Troll's Table, The	66148642
Trowlesworthy Bottom	566644
Tors (see Little & Great Trowlesworthy Tors)	
Warren	5764
Warren House	56776479
Waste	572632
Trumpetor	77897649
Tucker's Hill	643631
Tucking Mill	75417062
Tunhill	72707579
Road	72737570 (E)
Rocks	731758
Tunnaford	68936870
Tunnel Falls	50368395
Turf Hill	673832
House	56908064
Road	64307931 (NW)
Turn Teign	65008654
Turpin's Pit	620848
Twist	52767820
Two Barrows	70617920
Bridges	608750
Bridges Bottom	573782
Bridges Hotel	60907499
Brothers Adit	59106816
Burrows	70617920
Crosses in Turfe	70777631
Day Pond	56996884
Hills	678695
Oaks	70256746
Stones	65258545
Stones	74707704
Thorns X	67817092
Waters	63398390
Waters Hill	629838
Twyste Lane	52267783 (ENE)
Tyrwhitt's Wharf	51726511
Tythingland	51057210

U

U Stone	64456490
Udal Tor (see Roborough Rock)	
Ugborough Beacon	66855911
Moor	6561
Ullacombe	78387774
Uncle Ab's House	65626395
Uncle's Road	57837006 (E)
Underhill	65935688
Underhill	69876085
Cottage	51517395
Union Inn	75318610
Uphill	69897410
Uppacott (see Higher Uppacott)	
Cottages	73318830
Cross	73938861
Uppacott Down	735892
Farm	73388851
Farm	70127282
Hill	727887
Uppaton	61505810
Upper Dean	72906460
Leigh	78418803
Plantation	706727
Weir Pool	74106793
Upperton	76429031
Farm	79729013
Wood	763901
Urgles	53506491
X	53506487

V

V Stones	67558136
Vag Hill	680730
Warren	6772
Vaghill Pit	676723
Vags Hill	662621
Vale Down	526863
Valley of Rocks	559901
Varracombe (see Great Varracombe)	
Brook	620849
Vearge's Stream	695709
Vellake	551899
Corner	55609037
Down	553903
Ford	55629037
Gate	55019073
Newtake	553903
Venford Bottom	683706
Brook	671704
Reave	68047077 (E)
Reservoir	685709
Venn	50707310
Venn	83288690
Bungalow	51037350
Venney Ford	67537583
Ford Gate	67507581
Ford Marsh	675759
Lake	559695
Venneylake Farm	56266933
Venton	72107606
Venton	69499103
Bridge	71997661
Venville Stone	52437383
Vergyland Combe	595868
Vete Mill	73559160
Vicarage Bridge	61406030
(mis-named Wisdome Bridge on map)	
Hill	612602
Hill Head	609612
Victoria	76607827
Inn	(?)
Mine (see Druid Mine)	
Vidlin's Corner (see Beatland Cross)	

Vigers Corner	67996470
Vinneylake Farm	56206933
Hill	562693
Vitifer Dry	68168096
Mine	6880
Mine Leat (see Birch Tor & Vitifer Mine Leat)	
Vixen Tor	542742
Cottage	54247415
Ford	54077406
Newtake	5474
Plantation	544740
Voghill Lake (see Vogwell Lake)	
Vogwell Cottage	72018210
Down	723810
Farm	72238170
Lake	728810
Vomeborough (see Old House Hill)	
Vur Tor	588831
(mis-spelt Fur Tor on map)	
Brook	588820
Ford	58358379
Plain	580840
Wood	592834

W

Wacka Tor	662621
Wadley Brook	735855
Wain Tor (see Little Mis Tor)	
Wakeham's Rook	60686076
Waldron Farm	59637470
Walkham River	580811
Head	584810
Head Cut	578815 (W)
Head Peat Works	570807
Spur	572783
Valley Mine	49007080
Walkhampton	533697
Common	5772
Common Reave	57827306 (SW)
Consols	52156976
Inn	53316975
Wall Brook (see Hentor Brook)	
Walla Brook	676808
Walla Brook	544845
Walla Brook	625857
Walla Brook (see Hentor Brook)	
Wallabrook Bridge	65358711
Wallaford	72226582
Cross	72326562
Down	706658
Down Gate	71106573
Wallandhill	69308820
Walled Shaft Gully	67968103
Wallon	77359035
Brake	769901
Walna Building	670?79??
Wanford Wood	765810
Wapsworthy	53788019
Bridge	53728031
Brook (see Yoledon Brook)	
Common	5680
Wells	552882 (?)
War Cleave Wood	690879
Ward Bridge	54207201
Ware's Garden	58626432
Warren (see Ditsworthy Warren)	
Warmmacombe	68696777
Warmpit Copse	797817
Warn Bridge	72506472
Warne's Kitchen	53607260
Warner (see Walna Building)	
Warren Bounds	69508164
Bridge	72217221
Warren Cross	51377335
House Inn	67418095
House Pit (see Vaghill Pit)	
Path	48688109 (NE)
Plantation	61726010
Was Tor	50018295
Wash Gate	69376140
Washford Barn	69498827
Washing Place	65049325
Wastor Farm	49708278
Watchett Hill	615931
Cottage	61009328
Gate	61619331
Watching Place Cross	71298419
Watchmaker's Tomb	50908473
Water	759808
Cleave	763814
Hill	671813
Hill	765805 (?)
Oke Corner	68606598
Oke Plain	6965
Rock	76??80??
Rushes	744732
Turn	74267082
Watercombe	62446126
Gate	62506110
Waste	628611
Waterfield	74508743
Inn (now Watervale Farm)	
Waterfoot Clatter	680655
Waterleat Bridge	75307197
Wood	751721
Watermans Arms	73616613
Watern Combe	594669
Combe	625866
Down	636870
Ford	59206663
Ford	62598670
Hill	672813
Oke	565836
Tor	629868
Waters Down (see Water or Watern Hill)	
Meet	60729414
Watervale Farm	51858371
Wood	503836
Waterworks Hill	683713
Watery Lane	52296916 (SW)
Waverley	74697231

Way	68948992
Down	689892
Waye	76957195
Barton	68868695
Down	824832
Farm	77628124
Farm	76807185
Plantation	769723
Waytown Cottage	54427160
Weatherdon Hill (see Wetherdon Hill)	
Webb's Marsh	646792
Weddicott Cross	70498598
Wedlake	552782
Bottom	537773
Combe	542778
Crossing-Place	547782
Farm	53807743
Newtake	543777
Week Cross	72688511
X	71168653
Down	712864
Ford	66197242
Weeke Barton	82208795
Weekford Mills (see Beara House and the Mill)	
Weekmon's Stone	63358947
Weir Bridge	49277543
Pool	74126778
Well Farm	68429078
Park	58306617
Park	66626679
Wella Brook	665682
Bridge	66716705
Gert	665680
Stone	66466857
Wellaby Gulf	65917011
Wellpark	72766360
Wellpritton	71607040
Wellsfoot Island	70557015
Welltown	54067004
Welstor	74307300
Common	738730
Cross	73967210
Lodge	73997250
Rock	73707301
Wembley Walk	55186851 (SSE)
West Beam Mine (see Ashburton United Mine)	
Cleave	608940
Cleave Rocks	60909408
Combe	53188849
Combe	68328712
Combeshead	64125833
Coombe	70958251
Coombe Gate (see Coombe Gate)	
Coombe Stream	703817
Cottages	67228069
Down	543635
Down	77919120
Ford	71909170
Glaze Brook	660614
Goosesford	67539171
Horridge	76107414
Lodge	72507923

West Mil Tor	58759099
	(mis-spelt Mill on map)
Mill Tor (see West Mil Tor)	
Ockment	602860
	(mis-spelt Okement on map)
Okement (see West Ockment)	
Peeke	66205741
Rook	60196075
Rook Gate	60376130
Rook Leat	60896203
Shallowford	69207560
Sortridge Consols	49007080
Stoke	69407101
Underdown	70539131
Vitifer Mine	67908275
Webburn	691814
Week (see West Wyke)	
Wheal Friendship	48307965
Wheal Robert	510707
Withecombe	69769005
Wyke	65659260
Westabrook	76397480
Westabrook	75197045
Bridge	76437483
Farm	75207066
Westacombe Farm	79079014
Westcombe Down	706823
Westcott	78958695
Farm	70998763
Wood	785872
Western Beacon	654575
Corndon	69098499
Corner	64257460
Red Lake (see Homer Red Lake)	
Wella Brook	665683
Whitaburrow	65356549
White Barrow (see Western Whitaburrow)	
Wood	538715
Westlake	61019470
Wetherdon Hill	651589
Wheal Ann (see Devon United Mine)	
Ann Bottom (see Whealam Bottom)	
Betsy	51028139
Caroline	668808
Chance	59557001
Cumston	672723
Dorothy	659660
Dorothy Leat	65??67??
Eleanor	731833
Emily	650930
Emma	715675
Emma Leat	62237096
Forest	561912
Fortune	549755
Fortune Leat	55607769
Franco	505702
Frederick	546854
Friendship	506794
Friendship Leat	54978300
Gatepost	51427417
George	52957040

Wheal George	559857
Hazel	728710
Jewell	527813
Jewell Leat	53908450
Jewell Reservoir	523815
Katherine	61066851
Lucky	584735 (?)
Lucky	572748
Lucky	58?68?
Mary Emma	533852
Mary Emma Ford	53298519
Prosper	57357934
Rose	52156976
Ruth	598682
Surprise	51407402
Unity (see Hooten Wheals)	
Virgin	614884
Virgin Stone	61238837
Whealam Bottom	615698
Bottom Stream	617694
Hill	613698
Wheatfield	72008835
Whetcombe Bridge	84508160
Whiddon Deer Park	723894
Down	6892
Farm	72048893
Goyle	67729265
Mine	758721
Park House	72108924
Scrubbs	755716
Wood	728896
Wood	754721
Whidley House	80608910
Whimington	52327140
Whinfield	70326092
Whingreen	61835836
Whisky-and-soda Wood	683635
Whisselwell Farm	79407758
Whit Hedges	687690
Moor Circle	63268960
Moor Mead	633888
Moor Stone (see Whitmoor Stone)	
Ridge	648822
Tor	542787
Whitaburrow	56867930
Whitchurch Common	5374
Down	505737
White Barn	72909235
Barrow (see Whittaburrow)	
Bridge	60039192
Gate	57907596
Gate	74177615
Gate Cross	69498880
Hart	75308602
Hill (see Big Whit Hill)	
Hill	534838
Hill	674778
Hills	5663
Horse Inn	75268602
Horse Inn (now Castle Inn)	
Lady Waterfall	50108351
Moor	633892

White Pits	629898
Ridge	647822
Rock	573?730?
Thorn Inn	54196309
Tor (see Whit Tor)	
Water	701896
Wood	693718
White-Oxen Manor	72376189
White's Babeny	66117625
Slade	66117625
Whiteabury Cottage	72008853
Cross	72038849
Whitehorse Hill	6185
Hill Peat Pass	620855 (W)
Leat	62448330
Whitemoor Marsh (see Whitmoor Marsh)	
Whitenknowles Rocks	585672
Settlement	585670
Whiteoxen Arch	74076728
Whiteslade (see White's Slade)	
Whitestone	50797850
Whiteworks	613710
Whitey Cross	70426831
Mead	648650
Works	639887
Whithedges	687690
Whitmoor Marsh	651891
Stone	63358947
Whitstone	(?)
Whittaburrow	753752
Whooping Rock	72958228
Whortleberry Rock	751?768?
Wickford Mead	65807270
Widecombe Hill	727768
Widecombe-in-the-Moor	718768
Wider Brook Clitter	660655 (?)
Widey Glaze	575908
Widgery X	53988555
Wigford Down	5464
Clay Works	553650
Wigney	57109343
Wild Goose	67647650
Tor	623877
Tor Clitter	627876
Tor Ridge	620873
Tor Well	62728762
Wildbanks Corner	61928041
Hill	6180
Newtake	617800
Rocks	611802
Wilford Bridge	79857970
Wilkey's Moor	63045854
Will	53338146
May's House	63908671
Willa Brook	593650
(mis-named Hentor Brook on map)	
Willabeam	594701
Willaby Spring	59407012
Willake	53096476
Willandhead	679842
Willcock's Dyke	622708
William Crossing, grave of	50977878

William Crossing Memorial	62706791
Donaghy Memorial	64008000
Stone	77127790
Wiliam's Well	73567511
Willings Hill	5864
House	58806381
Walls	5865
Walls Circles	585645
Walls Reave	58236441 (N)
Walls Warren	5865
Willingstone	75358880
Cottages	75428905
Plantations	759891
Rock	75308872
Willis Cross	79977530
Willmead	79508111
Willow Stream	58027004
Willsworthy (see Higher Willsworthy)	
Bridge	53398167
Brook	545838
Butts	531834
Camp	523833
Ford	53918155
Gate	51788350
Lane	53398168 (NW)
Pound	53398168
Rifle Range	527833
Willy Corner Gate	69??63??
Wilminstone Hall	49537633
Wilmotts Mill	63899405
Wilsetton Farm	52037310
Wilsworthy	80137645
Win Ford	66267572
Steps	66267572
Wind Tor	708758
Windhill Gate	81908702
Windmill Hill (see Huxton Corner)	
Windwhistle	70697490
Windypost	53477430
Winford Brook	657758
Wingstone	74708108
Winneys Down	6281
(mis-placed on map)	
Brook	628818
Peat Pass (see Stat's House Cut)	
Traw	630816
Winscombe	73679213
Lane	73599158 (N)
Winter Tor	60989159
Wisdome Bridge	61436087
(name mis-placed on map)	
Farm	61606035
Mill	61486088
Wisedom Cottages	72269060
Wishing Pool	66806039
Wistmans Warren	612778
Wood	6177
Wood Ford	60707806
Withecombe Bottom (see Deep Valley)	
Cross	69628931
Withill	54867265
Withy Bed Mires	57??65??
Withy Tree Clitters	620772
Wittaburrow (see Whittaburrow)	
Witz End	77997226
Wo Brook (see O Brook)	
Wollake	627690
Ford	62826669
Hill	6267
Mire	627689
Wolleigh	80607984
Wonson, The (see Northmore Arms)	
Wonson	67508969
Manor	67468969
Mill Bridge	67818900
Wood Corner	78359142
Down	636862
Hole Pit	639860
Hole Stream	633857
(mis-named Hugh Lake on map)	
Lake	633857
(mis-named Hugh Lake on map)	
Pits	712794
Pits Stream	710795
Stone	63??86??
Wood-in-the-tor	54797380
Woodash	767809
Woodbrooke	77579090
Woodclose	57759441
Woodcock Hill	556876
Wood	787879
Woodencliff Wood	758714
Wooder Goyle	712788
Goyle Stream	712787
Lane	71647706 (NW)
Manor	71957771
Rocks	712789
Woodgate Cottages	80207510
Woodhouse	79327637
Cross	79437641
Woodland Copse	680884
Hill	547693
Wood	529798
Woodlands	81138788
Woodman's Corner	52756845
Woodpark Plantation	705872
Woodstone Gate	72068025
Woodtown	71598670
Woodtown	53997178
Woola Plain	682638
Quarry	68056372
Woolholes	682638
Wooston	76498899
Castle	765897
Down	766897
Gate	76??88??
Workman's Bridge	68347068
Ford	68347068
Gert	684702
Worm Hill	714845
Wormhill Bridge	72168488
Farm	71638465
Wortha	48678077
Mill	48548030

Wortha Mill Bridge	48478023
Wotton	72706646
Wrangaton	67805795
X	67675789
Gate	67405815
Golf Links	666582
Wray Barton	77058463
Brook	773849
Cleave	775843
Cleave Wood	773848

Yadsworthy	63186077
Waste	639608
Yalland	69116283
Cross	69106270
Warren	693633
Waste	69??62??
Yannadon Crags	55036794
Yar Tor	678740
Yard	73318372
Gate	52998160
Yarder	738753
Yardworthy	67908512
Common	677846
Yarner	775782
Beacon	77??78??
Copper Mine	782784
Lodge	78307808
Wells	775782
Wood	7878
Yarningdale	76508655
Yarrow Mine	783783
Yartor Down	677732
Yealm	614649
Falls	61736371
Rings	623624
Rocks	61686391
Steps	61736371
Yearlick Ball	567778
(mis-named Greena Ball on map)	
Gert	563776
Yelfords	67408670
Yellam	71468700
Yellands	69808537
Yellands	47398113
Cross	69838518
Yellowmead	56647424
Circle	57536787
Combe	573680

Zeal	67916260
Bridge	67936258
Burrows	677631
Cottage	67896242
Gully	676648
Head	647937
Head Cross	64829378
Hill	675635
Plains	6764

Wray Mine	771848
Wrayland	79078150
Barn	79078150
Wrey Consols	716684
Wreyland	78738105
Wringworthy HIll	498766
Writelan Stone	78588152
Writenol	76347831
Wydemeet	64797311
Wythrom, The	66356127

Y

Yellowmead Down	577679
(name mis-placed on map)	
Farm	57106775
Ford	56107455
Ford	59518316
Gate	57226797
Gert	57566770
Hill	5282
Lane	57226797 (SW)
Yelverton	523678
Reservoir	55026833
Yennadon X	54506942
Crag	54946759
Down	5468
Mine	552683
Yeo	79107326
Yeo	67858656
Bridge	67918651
Cotts	61436075
Farm	55106695
Mill	67868656
Mill Leat	67968628
Yeo, The (see Ashburn)	
Yeoland Consols Mine	520662
Yes Tor	581902
Yes Tor	56447247
Bottom	566725
Brook	572738
Ford	57979122
Green	557726
Yoleden Brook	563796
Yonder Dry Lakes	660704
Tor (see Little Fox Tor)	
Youlden	73388493
Brook (see Yoleden Brook)	
Youlditch	52157671
Youlditch	52309205

Z

Zeal Pool	68??62??
Tor Tramroad	67806300 (NW)
Warren	677631
Zempson	71226290
Bridge	71226270
Cross	71556290
Zoar	52408065
Down	524808

APPENDIX I

Prehistoric and Industrial Archaeology Sites:

Dartmoor has the highest concentration of Bronze Age remains in Western Europe, and its landscape has also been fashioned by past activities associated with the tinning industry. Aside from the magnificent scenery, itself, it is these two facets of Dartmoor's history which most attract visitors to the National Park. However, by far the majority of these remains bear no proper name and thus, by definition, are excluded from the main section of this guide, so the following lists of sites will hopefully prove to be of considerable assistance to would-be 'explorers'. The lists are by no means exhaustive, but contain the most important and best-preserved sites and can serve as a useful starting point to seeking out some of these remains. For more complete and authoritative information on these locations, users are recommended to refer to Butler's four volumes on Dartmoor Antiquities, as well as other books listed in the bibliography.

(In the following lists, locations are entered in grid square order from south to north and west to east; all sites listed are on public access land).

(a) **Prehistoric Sites**
KV = kistvaens; SR = stone rows; SC = stone circles; ST = settlements, hut circles, pounds; LS = longstones

539772 ST
539778 ST
542649 ST
54426440 KV
542787 ST
54707870 KV
549833 ST
555749 SRX2 LS KV ST SC
55637820 SC
55037873 LS
550825 ST
56486550 SC
56606578 KV
565835 ST
57506398 SR
57646398 SC SR
57536787 SC

576717 SR
576715 ST
588638 ST
58506365 LS
585645 ST
58476447 KV
58226520 KVx2
587693 SR SC
58806970 KVx2
594634 ST
59606588 KV
591669 SRx3 LS
59617962 LS
60757049 KV
60497393 KVx3
60517869 KV
61236640 KV

61807031 KV
61307355 KV
61047442 KV
61157440 KV
61239283 SC
623624 ST
62407018 KV
62337116 KV
62017207 KV
62087232 KV
62117242 KV
62607788 KV
632623 SR
63506442 SC SR
637656 ST SR
63786607 KV SR
63157214 KV
63907606 KV
63677948 KV
63907966 KV ST
635799 ST
637802 ST
63898313 SCx2
63268960 SC
63358947 LS
64465929 ST
64506035 KV
641652 ST SR
643577 SRx2 KVx4 SC ST
643916 SR

656585 SR
65495828 LS
65785932 KV
65985920 LSx2
65426073 LS SR
655611 SR
65217538 LS SR
65448110 KV
65508411 SC SR
659860 SRx3 SC LS
65488739 SC
66086081 SR
667661 ST
661826 SR
66808431 KV
660856 LS SR
669858 ST
668868 ST
67156300 ST
679644 ST
67817176 KV
673825 SR
68177384 KV
68998083 SR
701809 ST
73407550 KV
738759 ST
74107876 KV
74788835 LS

(b) **Tinners' Buildings and other Mining Remains**
TM - tinners' mills (stamping and/or blowing mills); TH = tinners' huts; TC = tinners' caches; WP = wheel pits; BD = buddles, dressing floors etc; MB = miscellaneous buildings (the last three categories at more recent mining sites)

49507047 MB
51107849 MB
51197853 MB
51207909 MB
51028139 MB
53527570 TH
533852 MB WP BD
539871 TCx5
549755 BD WP
54598535 WP BD MB
54158754 TC
54358784 TC
54428799 TC

55287546 TM
55307620 TM
55207663 TM
55988648 TC
56766958 TM
56308426 WP
56969174 WP
573701 WP BD
57497161 TM
57357934 MB WP BD
57788742 TH TC
58666842 TC
58746842 TC

58016856 TM
58616992 TH
59376676 TM
592677 MB
59156749 WP
593679 MB
59276995 WP TC
59507096 TH
59767028 TH
59557001 WP BD MB
59438662 TH
59038762 TH
60606364 TH
60166990 TH
60647833 TH
61706385 TM
61766351 TM
61066851 WP
61566940 TC
615708 MB WP BD
61557972 TH
614884 MB BD
61928963 MB
629676 THx2 TC
62786797 TH
62306976 TH
62497118 TH
62387113 TM
62777201 TH
62508660 TH
62088814 TH
62069201 TM
63956293 TC
63936509 TM
63928102 TH
63928144 TC
63808426 TM

64616807 TH
64247190 TH
64347183 TC
64687280 MB
64487279 TM
64088784 TCx2
65456692 TM
655708 MB BD
65387031 TH
65697113 MB
66826031 TM
66216350 WP
66306345 MB
66496327 TC
66586650 WP
66017110 WP
66187231 TMx2
67026305 TC
67908086 WP
67908275 WP BD
68887910 BD MB
68557971 BD
68887910 BD WP
68458002 MB
68338012 WP
68288031 MB
681809 MBx3
68198096 WP MB
68058110 WP
69428009 WP
69588112 TH
70166585 WP
70868232 BD
76657583 WP BD MB
76487596 MB
77098483 W BD MB

★★★★★

APPENDIX II

Some Useful Addresses and Telephone Numbers:

DARTMOOR NATIONAL PARK AUTHORITY
Parke, Haytor Road, Bovey Tracey,
Newton Abbot TQ13 9JQ
Tel: 01626 832093

THE HIGH MOORLAND VISITOR CENTRE
Old Duchy Hotel, Princetown,
Yelverton PL20 6QF
Tel: 01822 890414

DARTMOOR NATIONAL PARK VISITOR CENTRE
Museum Courtyard, West Street,
Okehampton EX20 1HQ
Tel: 01837 53020

MUSEUM OF DARTMOOR LIFE
Museum Courtyard, West Street,
Okehampton EX20 1HQ
Tel: 01837 52295

IVYBRIDGE (SOUTH DARTMOOR) TOURIST INFORMATION CENTRE
Leonards Road, Ivybridge
Tel: 01752 897035

DARTMOOR LIVESTOCK PROTECTION SOCIETY
Membership Enquiries:–
The Old Mill, Charlecombe,
Combe-in-Teignhead, Newton Abbot
TQ12 4RE

Help for sick or injured animals:-
Buckfastleigh (Tel: 01364 643411)
Haytor (Tel: 01364 661332)
Mary Tavy (Tel: 01822 810303)

Plymouth (Tel: 01752 260067)
Plymouth (Tel: 01752 880626)
South Brent (Tel: 01364 73121)
South Brent (Tel: 01364 72174)

THE DARTMOOR RESCUE GROUP
For Information, Membership Enquiries etc:-
Tel: Newton Abbot (01626) 62849

For Emergency Assistance:-
Dial 999 and ask for Dartmoor Rescue

THE DARTMOOR PRESERVATION ASSOCIATION
Central Office:-
Old Duchy Hotel, Princetown,
Yelverton PL20 6QF
Tel: 01822 890646

Hon. Membership Secretary:-
Mr. E. W. Luscombe, 10 St. Michael's Terrace,
Stoke, Plymouth PL1 4QG

MINISTRY OF DEFENCE — MILITARY RANGES FIRING TIMES
Tel: Exeter (01392) 70164
Tel: Okehampton (01837) 52939
Tel: Plymouth (01752) 701924
Tel: Torquay (01803) 294592

DEVON BUS SERVICES HELP-LINE
Tel: Exeter (01392) 382800
Tel: Plymouth (01752) 382800

COUNCIL FOR NATIONAL PARKS
45 Shelton Street, London WC2H 9HJ
Tel: 0171 240 3603

COUNTRYSIDE COMMISSION
South West Regional Office
Bridge House, Sion Place, Clifton Down,
Bristol BS8 4AS
Tel: 0117 973 9966

DEVON COUNTY COUNCIL RECORDS
OFFICE
Castle Street, Exeter
Tel: 01392 384253

WEST DEVON RECORD OFFICE
Unit 3, Clare Place, Coxside,
Plymouth
Tel: 01752 385940

DARTMOOR LETTERBOXERS '100 CLUB'
Cross Farm, Diptford, Totnes TQ9 7NU
Tel: 01548 821325

APPENDIX III

The Country Code — How the visitor can help

Observe the Country Code; you will be helping to protect both landscape and livestock:

* Enjoy the countryside and respect its life and work
* Guard against all risk of fire
* Fasten all gates
* Keep your dogs under close control
* Keep to public paths across farmland
* Use gates and stiles to cross fences, hedges and walls
* Leave livestock, crops and machinery alone
* Take your litter home
* Help to keep all water clean
* Protect wildlife, plants and trees
* Take special care on country roads
* Make no unnecessary noise

BIBLIOGRAPHY

The following books have been consulted during the compilation of The Gazetteer, and all have provided information of one sort or another to a number of the sites and locations named:

BEACHAM, P. *Devon Buildings — an introduction to local traditions* (Devon Books, 1990)
BEARD, H. *Buckfast in Bygone Days: memories and photographs of an old Devon village* (Devon Books, 1991)
BREWER, D. *A Field Guide to the Boundary Markers on and around Dartmoor* (Devon Books, 1986)
BURT, R., WAITE, P. and BURNLEY, R. *Devon and Somerset Mines: Metalliferous and Associated Minerals 1845–1913* (Univ. of Exeter in assoc. with Northern Mines Research Group, 1984)
BUTLER, J. *Dartmoor Atlas of Antiquities Volumes 1–4* (Devon Books, 1991/94)
CROSSING, W. *Crossing's Amid Devonia's Alps* (David & Charles, 1974)
  Crossing's Guide to Dartmoor (David & Charles, 1965)
  Gems in a Granite Setting (Devon Books, 1986)
  One Hundred Years on Dartmoor (Devon Books, 1987)
  The Ancient Stone Crosses of Dartmoor and Its Borderland (Devon Books, 1987)
  The Teign — From Moor to Sea (Quay Publications (Brixham), 1986)
FLEMING, A. *The Dartmoor Reaves: Investigating Prehistoric Land Divisions* (B. T. Batsford Ltd., 1988)
GILL, C. (editor) *Dartmoor: A New Study* (David & Charles, 1970)
GOVER, J.E.B., MAWER, A. and STENTON, F.M. *The Place-Names of Devon* (Vols. 8 and 9 of the English Place-Name Society) (Cambridge University Press, 1930/31)
GREEVES, T *The Devon Tin Industry 1450–1750: An Archaeological and Historical Survey* (PhD Thesis) (University of Exeter, 1981)
  Tin Mines and Miners of Dartmoor: A Photographic Record (Devon Books, 1986)
HARRIS, H. *Industrial Archaeology of Dartmoor* (David & Charles, 1986)
HARRISON. *The Crosses of Dartmoor* (privately published monograph)
HAWKINGS D. J. *Water From the Moor: An Illustrated History of the Plymouth, Stonehouse and Devonport Leats* (Devon Books, 1987)
HEMERY, E. *High Dartmoor — Land and People* (Robert Hale, 1983)
  Walking Dartmoor's Ancient Tracks — A Guide to 28 Routes (Robert Hale, 1986)
  Walking the Dartmoor Railroads (David & Charles, 1983)
  Walking the Dartmoor Waterways: A Guide to Retracing the Leats and Canals of the Dartmoor Country (David & Charles, 1986)
HOUSDEN, M. and P. *Down Dartymoor Way: Pen & ink drawings of Devon's National Park* (Penmarran Publishing, 1990)
KINGDOM, A.R. *The Yelverton to Princetown Railway* (Forest Publishing, 1991)
PETTIT, P. *Prehistoric Dartmoor* (David & Charles, 1974)
QUICK, T. *Dartmoor Inns* (Devon Books, 1992)

RANSOM, B. *Dartmoor's Greatest Walk: A Guide to the Perambulation of the Forest of Dartmoor* (Devon Books, 1987)
RENDELL, P. (editor) *The Dartmoor Newsletter* (The Old Dartmoor Company, Bi-monthly)
RICHARDSON, P.H.G. *Mines of Dartmoor and the Tamar Valley after 1913* (Northern Mines Research Society, 1992)
ROBINS, J. *Follow the Leat — A Series of Walks on Dartmoor* (J.A.C. Robins, 1984)
Rambling On with John Robins (John Pegg Publishing, 1988)
ROWE, S. *A Perambulation of Dartmoor* (Devon Books, 1985)
STANBROOK, E *Dartmoor Magazine* (Quay Publications (Brixham), Quarterly)
STARKEY, F.H. *Dartmoor Crosses and Some Ancient Tracks* (F. H. Starkey, 1983)
WADE, E. A. *The Redlake Tramway and China Clay Works* (Twelveheads Press, 1982)
WESTLAKE, R and Gill, C. *Dartmoor* (David & Charles, 1987)
WOODCOCK, G. *Tavistock Yesterdays: Episodes from her History, Part 3* (G. Woodcock, 1987)
WOODS, S. H. *Dartmoor Stone* (Devon Books in assoc. with the Dartmoor National Park Authority, 1988)
WORTH, R. H. *Worth's Dartmoor* (David & Charles, 1971)

The 1:10,000 (6") scale and 1:25,000 (2½") scale Ordnance Survey maps have also been examined, as have various volumes of Reports and Transactions of the Devonshire Association.